The World Made New

WHY THE AGE OF EXPLORATION HAPPENED
& HOW IT CHANGED THE WORLD

Marc Aronson & John W. Glenn

NATIONAL GEOGRAPHIC

Washington, D.C.

CONTENTS

Bartolomeu Dias off the Cape of Good Hope in 1488 (from a recent painting). On this voyage, Dias became the first European to round the southern tip of Africa.

3

INTRODUCTION

"In 1492 Columbus sailed the ocean blue": year after year, students have recited this poem, but what comes after the first line keeps changing. Once upon a time, we all said that an Italian captain sailing on a Spanish ship "discovered" America, as if the Europeans landed on empty shores. This book takes a completely different view. To begin with, historians are no longer sure where Columbus was born. More importantly, we now understand that the voyages that began in 1492 altered the entire world. It was not just that a New World was added to European maps, but that the lives of people throughout the world began to change.

This book looks at the Age of Exploration with the widest possible view. It is not a history of Europeans, but of the whole world, coming into contact. When you really look at the Age of Exploration, it was not just Europeans tracking through the hills, forests, and cities of the New World. From the beginning, plants, animals, germs, even people from the New World were brought back to Europe, Asia, and Africa. Yes, European soldiers marched through Mexico, but at the same time, the American tomato came to Italy; the American potato, to Ireland; the American chili pepper, to India. This book looks back at the Old and New Worlds, just before they came into contact. In "Causes," you will find information about why Europeans came to the Americas and why the Americans responded as they did to the new people in their

Compass rose from an atlas published in 1544.

midst. The middle of the book, "What Happened," describes the crucial events of the age. Here you can read about the captains, soldiers, and priests who brought the Americas into contact with the rest of the world. They were astonishingly brave, tough, and ruthless. In the last section, "Consequences," you will see the effects of the Age of Exploration traced throughout the planet. This is a global view of a turning point in world history.

Choices

In this book you will often notice us saying "we are not sure" – for example, where Christopher Columbus was born, or how many people lived in the Americas in 1491 (see pages 42–43). That is not because we were lazy and forgot to check. Rather it is that, recently, historians have been re-examining evidence on these issues and making exciting new discoveries. Just as scientists keep changing our picture of the dinosaurs and how they lived, historians are rethinking the early history of the Americas. "We are not sure" is another way of saying, "here is an interesting question you may have a chance to study yourself."

In this book we have chosen to label geographical locations with their modern names, such as Mexico, or Florida, or Brazil. Of course, these were not the names used at the time, but we felt that the modern terms would make the book more useful for you, our readers. There are a few exceptions, when it is important to trace a route through the landscape as it was then known, but these are clearly labeled. Similarly, many modern historians prefer to use Inka, not Inca, or to label the Aztec as the Triple Alliance or the Mexica. These changes may eventually be adopted by everyone else, but we feel that using more familiar terms will make it easier for you to match information you find here to other sources.

WHY WAS THERE AN AGE OF EXPLORATION?

In **1491**, Ferdinand and Isabella were driving to reclaim all of Spain from the Muslims. In the Andes Mountains of what is now South America, Inca Tupac Yupanqui was the glorious ruler of the Realm of the Four Quarters. As the Christians drove towards the last Muslim stronghold in hot, dry southern Spain, and as the Inca tightened their hold over the high mountains, each expected the next year to bring familiar challenges. They were wrong.

If there is one date that stands out in all of human history it is 1492 —the first encounter between advanced civilizations that had developed an ocean apart. In that year Columbus crossed the Atlantic bringing about change on a scale not one person on earth could have imagined.

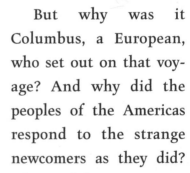

But why was it Columbus, a European, who set out on that voyage? And why did the peoples of the Americas respond to the strange newcomers as they did? In order to understand these questions, we first have to look at both sides of the ocean, just before they met.

Aztec Sun Stone (opposite): This is a modern reconstruction of the massive, 12-foot wide, 24-ton Aztec Sun Stone found buried in Mexico City. It records the Aztec view of time as a repeating cycle in which the present echoes the past. By contrast, Christians base their calendars around one event, the birth of Jesus. Before Columbus, the calendars in the Old and New Worlds were based on completely different beliefs. Book of hours (above): Books of hours were popular devotional texts in Europe in the 15th and 16th centuries. They contained prayers for readers to recite at specific times on particular days in the church calendar. Beautifully illustrated examples, such as this book of hours from 1524, were often cherished family possessions, passed from generation to generation.

EUROPE SETS SAIL

Zheng He, the great Chinese admiral (photograph of a mural in Zheng's hometown, Kunyang, China).

THE TURNING POINT that led to Columbus's historic voyage actually took place in 1433. China had been sending one vast fleet after another out to ports in Asia and Africa. Guided by the able, seven-foot-tall admiral Zheng He, these were the largest, best boats in the world. Had the voyages continued, China would have been the master of the seas. But in 1433, the emperor of China decided that the trips were too expensive, and he stopped them.

That very same year, Gil Eannes, a Portuguese sailor, returned home in defeat. He announced that he could not sail past Cape Bojador, a terrifying point in Africa considered to be the end of the earth. His master, Prince Henry of Portugal, insisted that he try again. The following year Eannes succeeded. One ship after another followed him, until Portuguese ships rounded Africa and reached India. With Portugal in control of the new sea routes, Christopher Columbus sought another path to Asia, across the Atlantic.

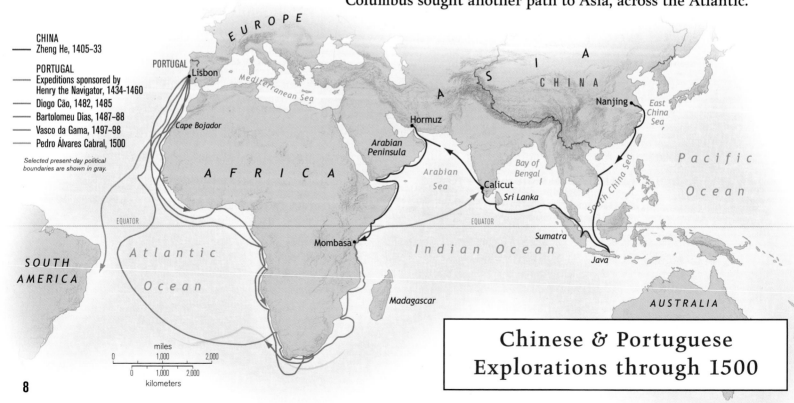

CHINA
— Zheng He, 1405–33

PORTUGAL
— Expeditions sponsored by Henry the Navigator, 1434–1460
— Diogo Cão, 1482, 1485
— Bartolomeu Dias, 1487–88
— Vasco da Gama, 1497–98
— Pedro Álvares Cabral, 1500

Selected present-day political boundaries are shown in gray.

EUROPE

PORTUGAL
Lisbon
Mediterranean Sea
Cape Bojador

AFRICA

ASIA

CHINA

Nanjing
East China Sea

Hormuz
Arabian Peninsula

Arabian Sea

Bay of Bengal

Calicut
Sri Lanka

South China Sea

Pacific Ocean

EQUATOR

EQUATOR

Mombasa

Indian Ocean

Sumatra

Java

SOUTH AMERICA

Atlantic Ocean

Madagascar

AUSTRALIA

miles
0   1,000   2,000

0   1,000   2,000
kilometers

Chinese & Portuguese Explorations through 1500

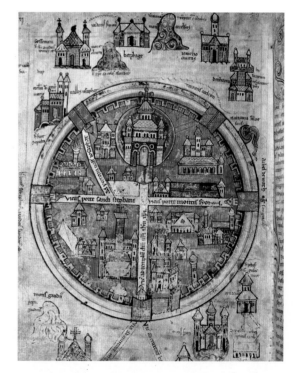

Christopher Columbus bids farewell to Queen Isabella of Spain as he sets off on his first voyage on August 3, 1492.

Columbus was not discouraged by the accomplishments of the Portuguese, just as Prince Henry refused to let Gil Eannes give in to his fears. Why were the Europeans so determined to voyage out into the unknown? They were hungry, but they did not lack food. Instead they treasured new knowledge. They were intensely competitive with each other. They craved wealth. They yearned for glory. And they felt a passion to spread their religion to the ends of the earth.

RELIGION

After the death of Mohammed in 632, Muslims conquered much of North Africa and the Middle East. In 711, Muslims invaded Spain. There were periods in Spain when Jews, Muslims, and Christians lived in peace. But in 1095, Pope Urban II urged Christians to fight a holy war to win back the Holy Land. In the 1400s Spanish Christians began their own crusade to purify Spain. On January 2, 1492, Granada, the last Muslim kingdom, fell to the Christian armies. All Jews were soon expelled. As Columbus set sail, believers in the most battle-hardened form of Christianity were flush with their recent victories and eager for new crusades.

Map of Jerusalem ca 1099 (above): The First Crusade, inspired by Pope Urban II, who urged Christians to conquer the Holy Land, culminated in the capture of Jerusalem in 1099. Less than 100 years later, in 1187, a Muslim army would retake the city.

COMPETITION

In China, whether or not a fleet sailed was entirely up to the emperor and his advisers. But when Columbus looked for sponsors for his plan to sail across the Atlantic, he went from one royal court to another. The kings, queens, and royal officers who listened to Columbus's proposal were eager to find a new route to Asia. However, the idea of sailing west across the Atlantic seemed far-fetched, and Columbus had a hard time convincing people that his plan could work. Portugal, which came close to backing him at one point, thought that sailing around Africa was more promising. But the courts of Europe were fierce rivals. Once Columbus claimed the New World for Spain, all of them wanted to send out their own ships to explore the new lands for themselves.

7th Century.	8th Century.	9th Century.
Muslim armies from Arabia conquer Syria, Palestine, Egypt, and North Africa.	From North Africa, Arab Muslims conquer Spain and Portugal and invade France.	Arab Muslim armies conquer Sicily and invade Italy; Ostia and Rome are sacked.

600   700   800   900

Rise of Islam and the Ottoman Empire

Christopher Columbus stands before King Ferdinand and Queen Isabella in February 1493, with Indians and treasure brought from the New World (19th-century print).

A view of Constantinople from a minaret (or tower) of the Ayasofya Mosque. Before the conquest of Constantinople in 1453 by the Ottoman Turks, the Ayasofya Mosque had been the Church of Hagia Sophia.

1492. Muslims expelled from Spain and Portugal by Christian armies, ending eight centuries of Islamic rule there.

1453. Constantinople falls to the Ottoman Turks. Muslims now control important Mediterranean trade routes to Asia.

1516. Syria and Palestine fall to Ottomans.

1529. Vienna unsuccessfully besieged by Ottomans.

1000	1100	1200	1300	1400	1500	1600

11ᵗʰ Century. Christian armies force Muslim conquerors out of Sicily.

1497–99. Vasco da Gama is first European to sail around southern Africa to the Indian Ocean; as others follow, the importance of Muslim-dominated Mediterranean trade routes is challenged.

1606. Ottoman Turks make peace with Austrians.

1571. In the battle of Lepanto in Greece, a joint Christian navy defeats the Ottoman fleet.

WEALTH

In 1453, the Ottoman Turks, who were Muslims, conquered Constantinople and renamed it Istanbul. Muslims now controlled all the known routes to Asia and could charge as much as they liked for the Asian spices and fabrics that were increasingly popular in Europe. These spices, including cinnamon, cloves, nutmeg, and pepper, were used by Europeans to improve the flavor of dried foods and disguise the taste of rancid food. They were grown naturally only in India, Sri Lanka, and in islands of what is now Indonesia. In the early 1400s, these spices were said to be worth their weight in gold. The country that could find a cheaper sea route to Asia would become immensely rich. This was the golden dream that sent the Portuguese around Africa.

A nutmeg merchant with his wares in 15ᵗʰ-century France (above, from a 15ᵗʰ-century manuscript). Nutmeg and other spices were in great demand in the 1400s, but before spices could reach the kitchens of Europe, merchants had to first transport them immense distances. Nutmeg, for example, was brought back from the Moluccas, or Spice Islands, in present-day Indonesia.

EUROPE SETS SAIL

King Arthur and the Knights of the Round Table, from a woodcut made in 1634.

Heroes and hunger: From the Age of Exploration to modern times, artists often depicted explorers as glorious heroes on epic adventures. The reality was usually harsher—arduous voyages plagued by disease, hunger, thirst, shipwrecks, and desperate skirmishes with suspicious native peoples. Here, Vasco Nuñez de Balboa dramatically claims the "South Seas" (the Pacific Ocean) for Spain in an engraving from the 19th century.

GLORY

While real knights set out across Europe on one campaign after another, poets in the castles of kings and queens were making up tales of legendary heroes on their own quests. From Spain to Germany, and from England to France, stories of King Arthur and Guinevere, of Roland, El Cid, and Siegfried were told and retold, and then set down in writing. These stories of great deeds, fearless men, and risk-filled journeys inspired explorers from the time of Columbus on. A captain sailing across the seas could easily picture himself as a knight on a heroic mission.

KNOWLEDGE

In 1415, Prince Henry of Portugal was part of an army that captured the Muslim port of Ceuta in North Africa. While in the city, Henry got a sense of the great resources in gold and slaves that Africa held. Three years later, determined to learn everything he could about the continent, he established a "school" where explorers, sailors, mapmakers, and astronomers shared their knowledge. As each captain sailed farther down the western coast of Africa, he reported back to the school, which made the next, longer, trip possible. Similarly, as soon as a captain returned from across the Atlantic, mapmakers scrambled to learn what he had found and to redraw their charts. Knowledge of the world was as precious as gold.

Vasco da Gama, from a 16th-century print. Building on the success of Prince Henry's school, da Gama led a trading expedition to India in 1497–99.

The sea quadrant: Invented in the mid-15th century, the sea quadrant helped sailors calculate their position at night relative to the pole star. This made sailing at night safer and allowed captains for the first time to make long journeys far from land (from an early 18th-century engraving).

EMPIRES OF THE AMERICAS

WHEN DID PEOPLE first come to what would later be called the Americas? Scientists are no longer sure. Every day new discoveries are challenging older theories. But this we do know: in the thousands of years that people lived in the Americas, they shaped the lands around them. Isolated from the rest of the world, the two continents became a vast agricultural laboratory.

Approximately 7,000 years ago, farmers somewhere in the Americas invented corn by carefully crossbreeding wild grains. Many of the vast stands of trees in eastern North America were planted sometime after A.D. 1000, selected for the nuts they yielded. High in the Andes Mountains of what is now Peru, farmers invented irrigation systems more efficient than those used today. Some scientists even think much of the immense Amazon rain forest was a kind of orchard created through generations of careful planting.

Hickory trees, similar to the plant at left, as well as other nut-bearing trees like beechnut, chestnut, oak (right), and walnut trees, were planted in great orchards by Indians in North America. In the 1600s, in part because of planting by Indians, as many as one in four trees in the eastern United States was a chestnut.

The Americans shaped the land to their needs. But there were limits. The last native horses died not long after people arrived in the Americas. Outside of llamas in the Andes, there were no large mammals to pull plows, carry riders, or share loads, nor were there any pigs or cows. With no horses, there were no cavalries.

In the Americas, rulers fought fierce battles against local enemies but had little sense of their more distant neighbors. The great Inca and Aztec empires, for example, were only just taking shape in 1492, and had not yet met. The Americans knew a great deal about how to use their land, but they had much less knowledge about how to deal with strangers.

Native American farmers in Florida, ca 1562 (from a late 16th-century hand-painted engraving). The drawing shows women working as farmers in the fields, which was quite common in the Americas.

THE INCA

"Worldshaker" was the name he gave himself, and he deserved it. Starting in 1438 the Inca leader Pachakuti carved out the largest empire on earth.

The lands Pachakuti and his sons ruled stretched thousands of miles along the Pacific coast of South America. That was like building a kingdom on top of a gigantic roller coaster, because from sea level the Inca lands rose straight up to the snow-capped peaks of the Andes. From what is now Ecuador to Chile, the Inca armies cemented their hold through conquest and intimidation. Only fear of the great Inca rulers and their soldiers could hold together such an immense empire.

Dressed and feathered Inca statue.

Machu Picchu, an Inca city perched high in the Andes Mountains. Historians believe that Machu Picchu was built around 1440, possibly as a retreat for Inca nobles.

ca 1438–1450. Inca emperor Pachakuti succeeds Viracocha in 1438 and expands the empire, dominating the central Andes and reaching Ecuador. A great fortress is built in Cusco in the 1440s, and Machu Picchu is built around 1450.

The Rise of the Inca

| 1200 | 1300 | 1350 | 1400 | 1450 |

ca 1200. The Inca tribe forms a small city-state in Cusco under the leadership of Manco Capac.

ca 1305. The Inca expand through the central Andes area.

ca 1350. War between the Inca and the Chancas.

ca 1390. The Inca are ruled by Viracocha, their eighth ruler and first empire builder.

ca 1470s. The Inca conquer Chímu and extend their reach into Bolivia, Chile, and Argentina. By 1493, the Inca have conquered the south coast of Peru.

Aztec farmers build a chinampa, or "floating garden" (16ᵗʰ-century illustration). In chinampa agriculture, Aztec farmers dug canals through swamps and marshy areas, piling the scooped-out mud onto beds of reeds. They would then plant their crops in the resulting mounds and even build their homes on them. Historians think the large population of Tenochtitlán was sustained, in part, by chinampa agriculture.

ca 1325. The Aztec establish Tenochtitlán city on two marshy islands in Lake Texcoco.

| 1300 | 1350 | 1400 | 1450 | 1500 |

The Rise of the Aztec

ca 1370. The first Aztec ruler, Tenoch, dies. Acamapichtli, the new ruler, expands the empire.

ca 1426–40. Aztec empire expands under a triple alliance linking the cities of Tenochtitlán, Texcoco, and Tlacopan.

ca 1440–68. Reign of Montezuma I, who conquers vast areas of Mexico. A huge temple is built in Tenochtitlán.

ca 1473–1502. The height of the Aztec empire. Tenochtitlán absorbs nearby city of Tlatelolco. In 1487, 20,000 people are sacrificed at the great pyramid in Tenochtitlán.

An Aztec priest offers a sacrifice of a victim's beating heart to the war god Huitzilopochtli. Aztec prisoners of war could expect little better than death or enslavement (from an Aztec illustration ca 1600–1650).

THE AZTEC

In 1400, the people who would come to be known as Aztec did not even rule the small region where they lived. In the next 30 years they fought their way to control of one of the richest, strongest, most powerful empires in the world. Tenochtitlán, the city of canals they built in central Mexico, was larger, cleaner, and more efficiently run than any European capital. The rivals of the Aztec would do anything to defeat them, even make alliances with invaders.

17

Birdman Tablet: This carved sandstone tablet, which shows a human dressed as an eagle, was discovered during an excavation on the Cahokia site in 1971.

THE LOST CITY

If the Europeans had reached North America in the 1100s instead of the 1500s, they would have seen a city that rivaled any in Europe. Cahokia, near St. Louis at the confluence of the Mississippi, Illinois, and Missouri rivers, was built around a 900-foot-long pyramid made of earth. Cornfields made it possible to feed the 15,000 people who gathered in Cahokia. But overuse of natural resources, climate changes that led to crop failures, and conflicts with other groups eventually devastated Cahokia, and the Americans scattered into small settlements. Archaeologists believe the people of Cahokia spread across the plains and prairie as well as to forests of the east, but they are not sure exactly which later groups can trace their roots back to the great city.

TRADE

Spread out across the mountains and valleys, forests and deserts of two vast continents, Americans developed many distinct ways of living. Though Cahokia fought battles and indeed rebuilt a log fortification around the center of their city four times, there were no movements like the Crusades, which united people all across Europe into one fighting force. But trade routes did connect groups separated by hundreds, even thousands, of miles. That is one way corn, which can only grow with human help, spread across the Americas. Americans learned from each other by handling seeds and tools from far away. No one in the entire world could have known that new objects can also carry new diseases.

Corn was a staple not only of the Secotan Indians in Virginia at the end of the 16th century (engraving ca 1590) but of native peoples throughout Central and North America.

THE EXPLORERS

The early years of Christopher Columbus are a complete mystery. All we know is that he, and the men who followed him, were determined to risk everything to sail across the ocean. No one could imagine what awaited them.

What young man herding his father's pigs could possibly know how he would behave should he come upon magnificent cities and an emperor in a room full of gold? How could he envision the rivers of blood that would follow his conquests? What student bending over ancient texts could picture green islands farmed by people missing from all history books? The men who became the explorers and conquerors of the New World did not know how cruel, or how brave, they could be until they climbed into their wooden ships and cast off to sea.

The Old World forged the will of the captains and priests who sailed away from its shores. That was enough to send them on their journeys. But it was in the New World that a frustrated sailor like Columbus, a swineherd like Pizarro, and a student such as Hernán Cortés stepped out of the anonymous ranks of their time and changed history.

American artist N.C. Wyeth painted The Romance of Discovery *(opposite) in 1943, 450 years after Columbus's voyage. Wyeth wants us to feel the drama of this historic moment. Compass rose (above): Decorative compass roses adorned many 15th- and 16th-century maps. Beginning with the topmost leaf, which points north, these blossomlike illustrations help map readers determine direction.*

On September 6, 1492, three boats guided by Christopher Columbus sailed off from the Canary Islands. He was on his way to Asia, carrying a letter of introduction to the Great Khan known to rule China. A month into the voyage, just after midnight of the moonlit October 12, a sailor named Rodrigo de Triana shouted "Land! Land!"

Columbus's coat of arms.

Pinta, Nina, *and* Santa Maria *(foreground) sail from Spain on August 3, 1492, as imagined in a recent painting.*

AUGUST 1492	SEPTEMBER 1492	OCTOBER 1492	NOVEMBER 1492

Columbus

August 9, 1492. Columbus reaches La Gomera in the Canary Islands; stays for a month to repair the *Pinta*'s rudder and lay in supplies.

November 21, 1492. Martín Alonso Pinzón sails off in the *Pinta* without permission to search for gold. Columbus, anxious to keep the peace in the remaining two ships, says nothing.

August 3, 1492. Columbus leaves Palos, Spain, in the *Santa Maria* (40 men) accompanied by two other ships, *Pinta* (26 men), captained by Martín Alonso Pinzón, and *Niña* (24 men), captained by Vincente Yáñez Pinzón (Martín's brother).

COUNTDOWN

1 **September 24, 1492.** Columbus soothes his men's growing distress at not seeing land for almost three weeks. The crisis passes, though there is talk among the crew of throwing Columbus overboard.

2 **Sunset, September 25, 1492.** Hopes are raised when an excited sailor shouts "Land!" But no land emerges.

3 **October 5, 1492.** Martín Alonso Pinzón quarrels with Columbus over the fleet's course; Columbus prevails and the ships continue westward.

4 **October 8, 1492.** With no further sightings, the frightened crew talks of turning back; a few days later, Pinzón gives Columbus three more days, after which they will sail for home.

5 **October 11, 1492.** Columbus pledges a silk coat to whoever sights land first, but the offer is met with silence by the distressed crew; birds normally seen near land pass near the ships; later that night, a trick of the light leads Columbus to think he's seen land.

6 **2 A.M., October 12, 1492.** With a cry of "Land! Land!" a lookout in the *Pinta* alerts the fleet to a distant coastline.

7 **Sunrise, October 12, 1492.** Columbus and his officers row ashore to an island, perhaps Guanahaní in the present-day Bahamas; he renames the island San Salvador and claims "the Indies" for Spain. The native peoples on the island are friendly to Columbus and crew; Columbus from the beginning refers to them as "Indians."

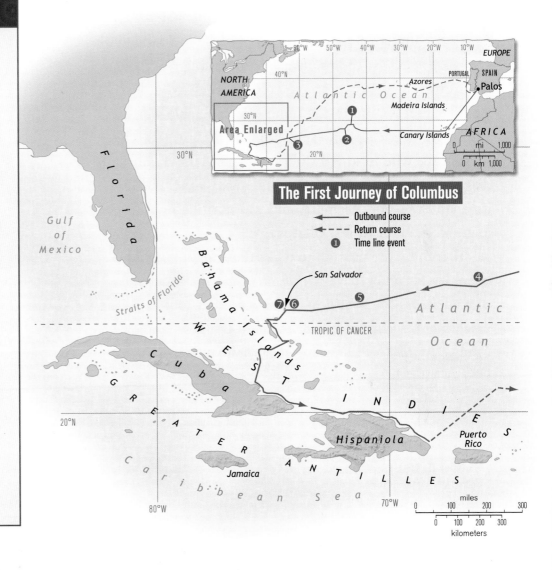

The First Journey of Columbus

→ Outbound course
--→ Return course
① Time line event

December 5, 1492. The *Santa Maria* and *Niña* sail for what Columbus soon calls La Española, or "Little Spain," now Haiti and the Dominican Republic. Columbus thought it was "the best land in the world."

January 1, 1493. Columbus sails for home in the *Niña*. He encounters Martín Alonso Pinzón and the *Pinta* near present-day Dominican Republic and pretends to accept his explanation for his disappearance.

Noon, March 15, 1493. *Niña* enters Palos harbor after 32 weeks at sea.

| DECEMBER 1492 | JANUARY 1493 | FEBRUARY 1493 | MARCH 1493 |

December 24, 1492. On Christmas Eve, the *Santa Maria* is wrecked on La Española. Columbus can't carry all his crew back on the *Niña* so he founds the town of La Navidad and leaves behind 39 men to hunt for gold and wait for the next Spanish expedition. This is the first European settlement in the New World.

In April 1493, Columbus arrives in Barcelona to a hero's welcome from the city and King Ferdinand and Queen Isabella. Though not all are convinced that he found Asia, his reports of a "new world" excite great interest throughout Europe.

THE AGE OF EXPLORATION

Columbus called the new people he met "Indians" because he was sure he had landed in the East Indies, near Japan. Having read books about travelers such as Marco Polo, he knew what he could expect to find in the Indies: fierce female warriors, men with dogheads who spoke in barks, cannibals. The Europeans who followed Columbus across the ocean began to realize that he was completely wrong. But if this land was not the Indies and was not filled with mythological creatures, what was it?

Driven by the passion to make their fortunes, and mercilessly competitive with each other, the Europeans spread across the Americas. Every step they took added new lines on maps, new stories about the new lands. And yet with new knowledge also came new myths.

Conquistador helmet from the 1500s. Armor gave the Spanish soldiers superior protection against most of the lighter weapons of the warriors they faced in the New World.

September 25 or 27, 1513. Vasco Nuñez de Balboa is the first European to see the Pacific from America.

October 12, 1492. Columbus reaches "the Indies." When word of his landfall reaches Europe, the great Age of Exploration begins.

1497–98. Exploration of Northwest Canada. Sponsored by the King of England, Italian-born John Cabot explores coasts of present-day Newfoundland in Canada.

September 6, 1522. The *Victoria* becomes the first ship to sail around the world when Juan de Elcano (del Cano) brings it in to Seville in Spain. The *Victoria* had set out on September 6, 1519, under Portuguese explorer Ferdinand Magellan, who was killed on April 27, 1521, on the island of Mactan in the Philippines.

November 15, 1533. Spanish conquistador Francisco Pizarro seizes the Inca capital city of Cusco, completing his three-year-long campaign to conquer the Inca empire. *(See page 28.)*

1535–36. French explorer Jacques Cartier is the first European to chart the St. Lawrence, one of the great rivers of North America, which he names after St. Laurens. *(See page 30.)*

1490	1500	1510	1520	1530	1540	1550

Age of Exploration

April 2, 1513. Ponce de León lands on east coast of Florida, naming the land "Pascua de Florida" (feast of flowers) and claiming it for Spain.

August 13, 1521. Conquistador Hernán Cortés takes control of Tenochtitlán, the Aztec capital city, completing his conquest of the Aztec Empire. *(See page 26.)*

April 17, 1524. Italian-born Giovanni da Verrazano, sailing for King Francis I of France, anchors near New York Bay–he is the first European to reach New York Harbor.

June 1541. MISSISSIPPI REACHED Spanish conquistador Hernando de Soto crosses the Mississippi near present-day Memphis, Tennessee, the first European to do so. *(See page 32.)*

As Hernán Cortés and Francisco Pizarro discovered, the Aztec and the Inca controlled astonishing stores of gold. How many more wealthy kingdoms were there? In South America, rumors told of a Golden Man, El Dorado, and his fabulous city of gold. In North America, there were said to be seven cities of gold. Whether it was Hernando de Soto in the Southeast, Jacques Cartier in Canada, or Walter Ralegh in Guyana, Europeans were willing to risk anything in the hopes of new triumphs. All these later explorers were chasing their own dreams. The "gold" they found was knowledge, not metal.

John Cabot and his son Sebastian make landfall on the northeastern Canadian coast, perhaps near Cape Breton, in 1497, as imagined in this 19th-century engraving. Cabot believed, like Columbus before him, that he'd reached Asia.

1560 · 1570 · 1580

1576–78. Englishman Martin Frobisher explores the Arctic Ocean, northeast Canada, and Baffin Island.

1585. Sir Walter Ralegh establishes the first English settlement in the New World–short-lived Roanoke in present-day North Carolina. *(See page 35.)*

Spanish explorer Ponce de León was just one of many European adventurers who pursued rumors of lost kingdoms or, in his case, the Fountain of Youth. Here, he is offered a drink of the legendary liquid that would allow men to live forever, as imagined in this later illustration. Though he led two expeditions to Florida, in 1513 and 1521, in search of the fountain, he never found it.

IN MARCH OF 1519, Hernán Cortés marched inland from the coast of Mexico to challenge the mighty Aztec empire. The Spanish had first heard of a wealthy civilization farther inland when Cordoba (in 1517) and Grijalva (in 1518) returned to Cuba from explorations of the Yucatán coast. Diego Velásquez de Ceullar, governor of Cuba, commissioned Hernán Cortés to explore further. In February 1519, Cortés left Cuba with 11 ships, 550 men, and 16 horses bound for the mainland. The battle between Cortés and the Aztec he encountered would be the first great contest for control of the New World.

April–July 1519. The Aztec emperor Montezuma sends Cortés gifts of gold and jewels but orders the Spaniard to stay on the coast. To make sure none of his men sail back to Cuba, Cortés hauls most of his boats out of the water.

February 18, 1519. Cortés sets sail for the Yucatán. From Mayas living on the coast, he hears of people rich with gold further inland. Cortés sails west and north along the coast hoping to make contact.

August 8, 1519. Cortés sets off inland, toward the emperor's capital, Tenochtitlán. On his march, Cortés is attacked at Tlaxcala but the Tlaxcalteca warriors are quickly overwhelmed. Enemies of the Aztec, they add 2,000 warriors to Cortés's force after he promises to destroy the Aztec.

1519

Cortés

March 4, 1519. Cortés lands in Tabasco, in present-day Veracruz State, Mexico, and names his landing spot Veracruz (True Cross).

November 8, 1519. Cortés arrives in Tenochtitlán. Montezuma and Cortés greet each other warmly. But Cortés soon takes Montezuma prisoner and demands a huge ransom in gold and an end to human sacrifice.

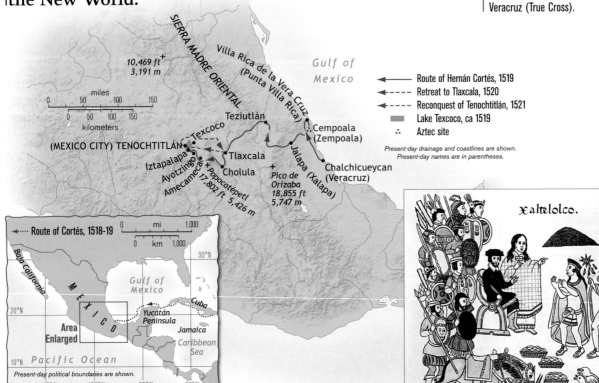

SIERRA MADRE ORIENTAL

10,469 ft
3,191 m

Villa Rica de la Vera Cruz
(Punta Villa Rica)

Gulf of Mexico

Teziutlán

Texcoco

Cempoala
(Zempoala)

(MEXICO CITY) TENOCHTITLÁN

Iztapalapa
Ayotzingo
Amecameca
Popocatépetl
17,802 ft 5,426 m

Tlaxcala
Cholula

Jalapa (Xalapa)

Pico de Orizaba
18,855 ft
5,747 m

Chalchicueycan
(Veracruz)

miles
0   50   100   150
0   50   100   150
kilometers

⟵ Route of Hernán Cortés, 1519
⟵--- Retreat to Tlaxcala, 1520
⟵--- Reconquest of Tenochtitlán, 1521
▪ Lake Texcoco, ca 1519
∴ Aztec site

Present-day drainage and coastlines are shown.
Present-day names are in parentheses.

Route of Cortés, 1518–19

0   mi   1,000
0   km   1,000

30°N

Baja California

Gulf of Mexico

MEXICO

Cuba

Yucatán Peninsula

Jamaica

Area Enlarged

20°N

Caribbean Sea

10°N   Pacific Ocean

Present-day political boundaries are shown.
110°W   100°W   90°W   80°W

Malinche, Cortés's Indian interpreter. Some Mexicans later viewed Malinche (standing to Cortés's left in this 16th-century illustration) as a traitor; others celebrated her as the mother of the new, mixed society.

Cortés and Montezuma meet for the first time on November 8, 1519 (19th-century print).

August 13, 1521. Cuauhtémoc surrenders. The Spanish take control of the city. Every building is razed; scarcely a trace of the old city remains. As many as 100,000 to 240,000 Aztec are estimated to have died during the siege and in the massacre that followed.

May–August 1521. Cortés lays siege to Tenochtitlán. Over the 93-day conflict, the Aztec suffer starvation and disease. But their resistance is ferocious and unyielding; thousands die trying to beat back the Spanish.

April 1520. Cortés departs for the coast after hearing that another Spanish force, sent by Velázquez, has landed to take over the expedition. Cortés leaves behind part of his force.

1520

1521

May 16, 1520. While attempting to stop a religious ritual, the Spanish are attacked and kill many Aztec. This leads to weeks of street skirmishes.

May 28–29, 1520. Cortés surprises the new Spanish troops in a night raid and persuades them to follow him. Cortés returns to Tenochtitlán to find his soldiers surrounded in their palace.

July 1, 1520. Cortés retreats from Tenochtitlán. Laden with gold, he and his men try to escape from the city at night but are ambushed. Half of the Spanish force is killed in what they call the Noche Triste (Sad Night). Cortés and the other survivors retreat to Tlaxcala.

December 27, 1520. Together with 150,000 local allies, including the Tlaxcalans, Cortés sets off to reconquer Tenochtitlán. Over the next several months, they take control of the towns and cities ringing the capital.

The loss of Tenochtitlán marked the end of Aztec rule. The Spanish claimed all of Mexico and Cortés began to build Mexico City over the ruins of Tenochtitlán. By 1540, Mexico City was the center of Spanish America.

June 30, 1520. Montezuma dies. Three days earlier he'd begged his people to make peace but was stoned by them. Cuauhtémoc becomes the last Aztec emperor.

Cortés sent this map of Tenochtitlán, prepared by Aztec artists, in a letter to King Charles V describing his conquest. When Cortés and his men reached the city they were awed by its size and beauty.

T he great success of Cortés in Mexico fired the imaginations of would-be conquistadores throughout Spain and the New World. Cortés proved that a small force of highly trained Spanish soldiers could win an empire. In 1528, along the Pacific coast, Francisco Pizarro captured an Inca trading vessel filled with gold and jewels. In December 1530, he set off to carve out his own empire.

Route of Francisco Pizarro, 1531–33
∴ Inca site

December 27, 1530.
Pizarro's third expedition sails from Panama.

Present-day political boundaries are shown.
Present-day city names are in parentheses.

1530
Francisco Pizarro

All Spanish soldiers wore armor of some kind, though usually only wealthy soldiers could afford a full suit, as shown in this late 16th-century illustration. In battle in the Americas, many conquistadores wore lighter chain mail shirts, or escaupli, padded cloth armor adopted from the Aztec.

Atahualpa (opposite) is seized by a Spanish soldier (19th-century print). When Pizarro arrived in Peru in 1532, the Inca emperor Huayna Capac had died of small-pox and a fierce civil war between his sons Atahualpa and Huascar was just ending. The empire was weak and divided and, once Atahualpa was captured, unable to effectively counter the Spanish.

The shields of Inca warriors were decorated with copper stars, such as this.

August 11, 1533. Pizarro sets out from Cajamarca for Cusco, the capital city, with the new Inca emperor Tupac Huallpa under armed escort.

May 16, 1532. Pizarro leaves Tumbes to explore northwest Peru. Hernando de Soto joins the expedition.

October 12–November 14, 1533. Spanish forces fight Inca warriors in towns along the route to Cusco and, finally, at a pass just above the capital city. During the march, Tupac Huallpa dies of illness.

November 8, 1532. Pizarro turns inland, marching into the Andes. He is met by an adviser to Emperor Atahualpa, who guides the Spaniards through the mountains to the emperor's camp.

1531. Pizarro lands on coast of Ecuador. He arrives in Tumbes in January to find it in ruins, a casualty of the Inca civil war.

November 15, 1533. Pizarro takes the Inca capital city of Cusco. Manco, a son of Huanya Capac, is installed as the new Inca emperor.

1531 **1532** **1533**

September 24, 1532. Pizarro marches out of San Miguel with 102 infantry and 62 horsemen and heads south, reaching Saña on November 6.

With the capture of Cusco, the main cities of the Inca Empire were under Spanish control. The viceroyalty of Peru quickly became an important center of Spain's colonial empire.

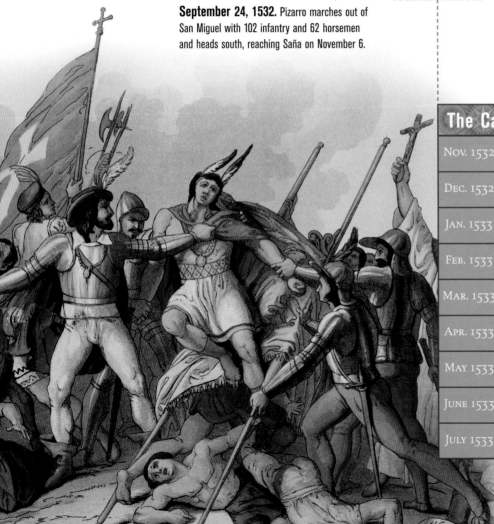

The Capture and Execution of Atahualpa

Nov. 1532 Dec. 1532 Jan. 1533	**November 15, 1532.** Pizarro arrives at Cajamarca, Peru, where Atahualpa is encamped with an 80,000-strong army; he sends his brother Hernando Pizarro and Hernando de Soto, along with 35 horsemen, to invite Atahualpa to a meeting.
Feb. 1533 Mar. 1533	**November 16, 1532.** Atahualpa visits Pizarro's camp and is ambushed; he is captured and the Spanish soldiers kill 6,000 Inca warriors. The next day, Atahualpa offers Pizarro a ransom: a room of gold for his freedom. Pizarro agrees, but while the Inca gather the treasure he sends a request to Panama for more troops.
Apr. 1533 May 1533	**April 14, 1533.** Spanish reinforcements (150 soldiers and 50 horses) arrive in Cajamarca from Panama.
June 1533 July 1533	**July 26, 1533.** The ransom paid, Pizarro executes Atahualpa, after hearing reports that Atahualpa was plotting his escape and secretly gathering an army to oppose the Spaniards. He installs Tupac Huallpa as Inca emperor.

Starting in 1479, unusually large catches of fish arrived in the English port city of Bristol. Europeans may already have known of Newfoundland and the rich fishing grounds nearby. If the lure of gold drew soldiers to the south, it was fish that pulled them to the north. Fish—and the dream of finding a northern sea passage to Asia. Starting in 1534, Jacques Cartier sailed a full thousand miles down what is now Canada's St. Lawrence river and established the French claim to North America.

Codfish drew English and French fishing boats to the waters off the coast of Newfoundland. Cod would later be called "New Foundland's Currency" (19th-century illustration).

Route of Jacques Cartier, 1535-36
International boundary
Provincial boundary
Undefined provincial boundary

Present-day political boundaries are shown.
Present-day names are in parentheses.

April 20, 1534. Cartier leaves France with 61 men and 2 ships. He explores the coast of Newfoundland, Prince Edward Island, and the Gulf of St. Lawrence.

May 19, 1535. Cartier, with 110 men and 3 ships, returns to North America and enters Newfoundland-Labrador waters through an opening called the Baye des Chastreaux (Straight of Belle Isle). He explores the inland sea beyond Brest.

October 2, 1535. Cartier continues upriver to Hochelaga, a large village of 1,000 Iroquois Indians; he names a nearby hill Mont Réal, near present-day Montreal.

September 1, 1535. Passes mouth of Saguenay River.

1534   1535

Cartier

September 5, 1534. Returns to France.

August 10, 1535. Cartier names a bay St. Laurens on the northern coast of the Newfoundland-Labrador waters (the name would soon extend to the great Gulf of St. Lawrence and the St. Lawrence River). Cartier explores around the mouth of the St. Lawrence River and then heads up river.

September 7, 1535. Cartier encounters the Iroquois Indians and visits Iroquois village of Stadacona, near the present-day Quebec.

An Iroquois Indian from the northeast (19th-century print). Cartier's encounters with the Iroquois along the St. Lawrence were friendly. He and his men spent the winter of 1536–37 in the Iroquois town of Stadacona, near present-day Quebec.

The city of Quebec, on the St. Lawrence River, ca 1688 (detail from a 17th-century map). Just 150 years after Cartier's daring exploration up the St. Lawrence, the city of Quebec had become an important trading center and foothold in North America for France.

QUEBEC
Comme il se voit du côté de l'Est

Cartier paddles up the St. Lawrence River in 1535 as a party of Iroquois looks on (19th-century engraving).

1536

Spring 1536. The expedition makes its way back to the gulf.

Winter 1535–36. Finding the river impassable beyond Mont Réal, Cartier returns to Stadacona, where he spends the winter. His men suffer terribly; 25 die.

June 1536. Sailing south down the Gulf of St. Lawrence, Cartier is the first European to locate a southern passage out of the gulf; he sails for France.

May 1536. Cartier captures seven Iroquois, including Chief Donnaconna.

Cartier would return to the St. Lawrence again in 1541 to prepare the way for a party of French settlers. Though this first French colony would not last, reports of Cartier's 1,000-mile journey up the great river and the rich land he saw inspired others to follow in his footsteps.

July 16, 1536. Arrives in France.

Beginning in 1539, Hernando de Soto marched his men, horses and pigs (for food) from Florida to the Mississippi in search of new conquests. While his men saw many people, great stores of corn, and mounds similar to Cahokia, they found no new gold. De Soto was a bloody, cruel leader who left behind a path of destruction. When Europeans returned to the Mississippi Valley 150 years later, the lands were empty.

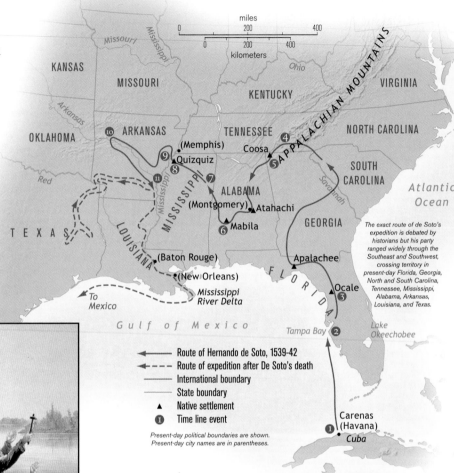

The exact route of de Soto's expedition is debated by historians but his party ranged widely through the Southeast and Southwest, crossing territory in present-day Florida, Georgia, North and South Carolina, Tennessee, Mississippi, Alabama, Arkansas, Louisiana, and Texas.

→ Route of Hernando de Soto, 1539-42
--→ Route of expedition after De Soto's death
— International boundary
— State boundary
▲ Native settlement
❶ Time line event

Present-day political boundaries are shown.
Present-day city names are in parentheses.

Hernando de Soto

6 **October 18, 1540.** De Soto's party fights a large force of Choctaw Indians near present-day Montgomery, Alabama, destroying the Choctaw fortress of Mabila and killing at least 2,000 Choctaw Indians; just 20 Spaniards are killed but most of de Soto's supplies are lost.

1539

1540

1 **May 18, 1539.** Hernando de Soto sets sail from Cuba for Florida in search of gold with 9 ships, 600–700 men, 24 priests, 220 horses, and a pack of fighting dogs.

3 **September 1539.** De Soto takes hundreds of Seminole Indians prisoner after the Battle of the Lakes. Throughout his two-year-long expedition, de Soto would fight one Indian tribe after another, forcing the native peoples he encountered to guide him through their lands and demanding they show him where to find gold.

4 **May–June 1540.** The expedition crosses Appalachian Mountains, the first Europeans to do so.

7 **December 1540–April 1541.** The expedition winters with Chickasaw Indians in present-day northeastern Mississippi.

5 **July 16, 1540.** De Soto enters the village of Coosa in present-day Georgia and stays a month, taking the village chief and his sister hostage.

2 **May 25, 1539.** De Soto arrives in Florida near present-day Tampa Bay and marches north.

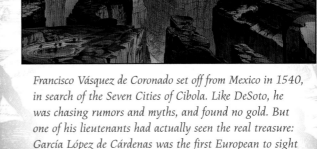

Francisco Vásquez de Coronado set off from Mexico in 1540, in search of the Seven Cities of Cibola. Like DeSoto, he was chasing rumors and myths, and found no gold. But one of his lieutenants had actually seen the real treasure: García López de Cárdenas was the first European to sight the Grand Canyon (19th-century illustration).

De Soto's men torture Indians for information about where to find gold (16th-century engraving).

1541

9 June 15, 1541. The expedition crosses the Mississippi River and continues westward into present-day Arkansas, Oklahoma, and Texas.

8 May 8, 1541. De Soto and his army are the first Europeans to sight the Mississippi River.

10 August 1541–March 1542. The expedition meets Plains Indians and is told about, but does not see, buffalo.

11 May 21, 1542. De Soto dies of a fever and is buried in the Mississippi River; by now, more than half of de Soto's original army has perished from constant conflict with native peoples or disease; rest of expedition continues to Gulf Coast and then to Mexico.

1542

De Soto's remarkable journey was marked by personal failure—he set out to find gold and never did. However, his wanderings pointed the way westward for future Spanish exploration.

By the end of the 16th century, the era in which the Spanish were finding one kingdom after another in Central and South America was giving way to another of British settlement in North America. The European powers were now often in direct conflict in the New World. The map from 1589 at the right charts English privateer Sir Francis Drake's raid on Spanish-held territory in the Caribbean in 1585–86. It also vividly illustrates why the great Age of Exploration was coming to an end. Where Columbus had steered west into the unknown, Drake in 1585 sailed along a well-traveled ocean "highway" that tied together Europe, Africa, the Caribbean, and the Americas. The Atlantic, once a forbidding ocean barrier, was now more like a familiar lake.

Secota, an Algonquin Indian village. This engraving from 1590 drew upon sketches made by John White, who led the Roanoke colony.

THE Famouse West Indian voyadge made by the Englishe fleete of 23 shippes and Barkes, wherin weare gotten the Townes of S. IAGO: S. DOMINGO, CARTAGENA and S. AVGVSTINES the same beinge begon from Plimmouth in the Moneth of September 1585 and ended at Portesmouth in Iulie 1586 the whole course of the saide Viadge beinge plainlie described by the pricked line Newlie come forth by Baptista B.

Drake's Caribbean Raid, 1585-1586

1585

1 **September 14, 1585.** Drake sets off from Plymouth, England, with a fleet of 29 ships.

2 **September–November 1585.** Drake's raiding party sails to the Caribbean along the route commonly used by Spanish ships in the late 16th century: south down to the Cape Verde Islands before turning west across the Atlantic.

3 **November 17, 1585.** Drake sacks Santiago in Spanish-held Cape Verde Islands.

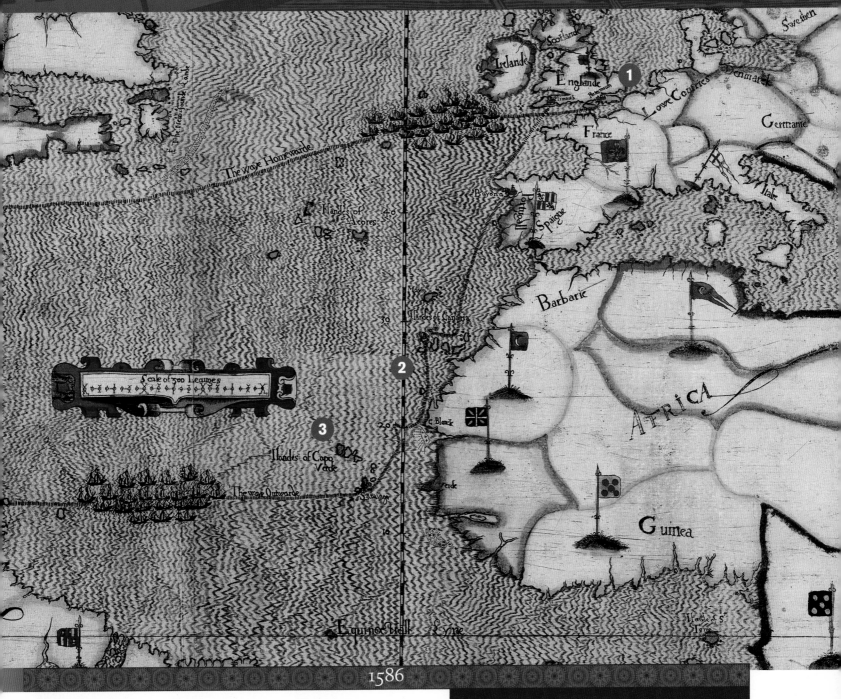

1586

4 November 29, 1585– March 26, 1586. The fleet sails from Santiago, crosses the Atlantic, and raids Spanish-held Santo Domingo and Cartagena in the Caribbean.

5 May 28–30, 1586. Drake captures and destroys St. Augustine in Florida.

6 June 1586. Drake stops at Roanoke Island, to check on the colony sent out by Sir Walter Ralegh the year before. The settlement is struggling; most of the colonists return home with Drake.

Drake's voyage was ambitious but did not succeed in significantly disrupting the Spanish. Similarly the colony Ralegh sent to Roanoke also failed. But Roanoke established a model for a future British settlement in North America. Jamestown, founded in 1607, was built on the very site Ralegh had envisioned for his earlier settlement.

HOW THE AGE OF EXPLORATION CHANGED THE WORLD

In the hundred years after Columbus, European soldiers slashed through South America, followed by priests, officials, merchants, and pirates. For the native peoples of the Americas, this was a period of unimaginable loss, as perhaps nine of out every ten died from disease, malnourishment, and abuse. Yet through the century something new was taking shape: Americans, Europeans, and Africans were mixing. They produced children of every color, established new forms of religion, created new ways of living. Hispanic America was beginning.

At the same time, the ships plying the waters from Europe to Africa, to Asia, to the Americas and back again did more than transport men and goods. Each ship was a kind of line drawn in space, connecting people, nations, and continents. Along those lines traveled animals, foods, germs, ideas, people, even fashions. No one was left untouched. What we call the Age of Exploration was really the beginning of the modern age of worldwide connection. Though the century of conquest left a terrible path of human suffering, it also created, for the very first time in human history, a world joined.

The Western Hemisphere ca 1600 (opposite and map detail above): Before Columbus, the most informed scholars, sailors, and geographers had no knowledge of the enormous land masses that stood between Europe and Asia. But after just a hundred years of exploration, European mapmakers began to understand the general shapes of North and South America, making true maps of the world possible for the first time in history.

Carib Indians of the West Indies (from a 17th-century illustration). Carib Indians migrated from South America into the West Indies beginning about 1400. Columbus reported meeting the Caribs on his first voyage. On some of the Caribbean islands, the Caribs managed to escape from the Europeans by living in the mountains. There, they intermarried with Africans who escaped from slavery.

IN 1491, NOT ONE PERSON in Italy had ever seen a tomato, nor was there a single potato in Ireland, a chili pepper in all of Asia, or a kernel of corn in Africa. In turn, no living American had ever ridden a horse, milked a cow, or eaten a bowl of rice. To get a sense of how dramatically the world changed in the following years, consider the island Columbus called Hispaniola.

In 1491, the island that is now Haiti and the Dominican Republic was home to perhaps 200,000 people. (For the reasons why this number is so hard to pin down, see pages 42–43.) Most of these people called themselves Tainos, though at the time of Columbus the Tainos were fending off invading parties of Caribs from nearby islands. The Tainos lived near the coast and ate fish, as well as other animals they could catch, such as snakes, bats, or birds. Fifty years later, there were fewer than 700 natives still living on the island. Instead, Spaniards ran sugar plantations where populations of up to 200 African slaves were common. Thirty-four mills had been built to process sugar cane, a reed that originally came from New Guinea and that Columbus had brought over on his second voyage. By 1530, 80 percent of the sugar used in Europe came from Hispaniola. An island that had been known only to the Taino and their local rivals was now a way station in traffic linking Europe, Africa, the Americas, and Asia.

Within the New World itself, people from Africa, Europe, and the Americas were forced together, and

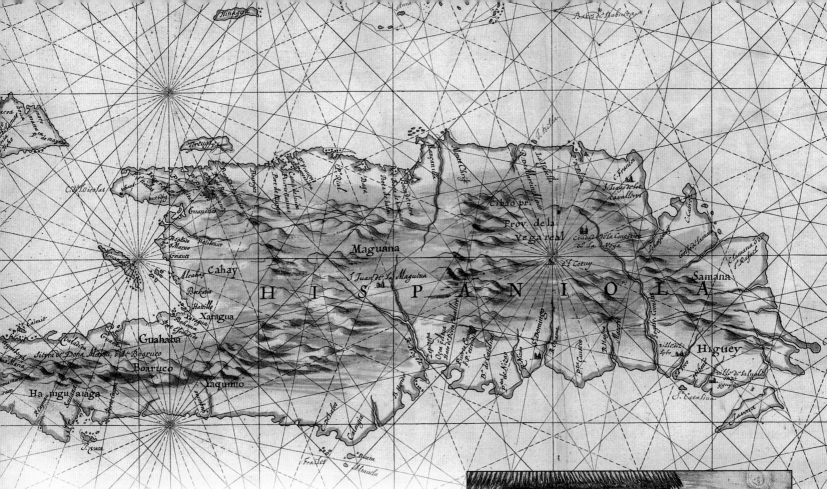

Map of Hispaniola, ca 1639, showing coastal features and towns. By the late 1500s and early 1600s, Hispaniola was a firmly established center of Spanish power, accurately depicted on most world maps and a familiar port of call for Spanish merchant ships.

had to adapt to survive. The children of the Aztec and Inca found ways to blend Christianity with their own gods. Sold from their homelands, Africans soon learned how to plant familiar crops such as plantains and yams in new soil. Europeans living thousands of miles from their birthplace experimented with new clothing styles and foods. The very newness of the new land even inspired all of these peoples to think in new ways. Was it necessary that a country have a king? Was it certain that the existing church spoke for God? The example of the New World soon brought with it these new questions.

African slaves at work in a sugar mill in Hispaniola in the early 1600s (engraving ca 1623). Before the Spanish came to the New World, sugar was so expensive that only very wealthy people could afford it. To create cheap sugar, Europeans needed many workers. When the Native Americans died off, enslaved Africans were brought in to replace them. Not only was the work punishing but the Spanish treatment of the African slaves was brutal.

A WORLD JOINED

DISEASE

The peoples of the Old World lived near cows, dogs, and pigs, which can transmit diseases such as measles and smallpox. Over thousands of years, people slowly built up some resistance to these illnesses. In the Americas there were no cows or pigs, indeed, there were few domesticated animals of any sort. This meant the Americans had almost no resistance to these diseases. Some historians estimate that in the centuries following Columbus as many as nine out of ten of the native people throughout the New World may have lost their lives to illness and other causes. There are now almost 300 million people in the United States. An epidemic of the same power would result in the deaths of 270 million people and leave an empty land.

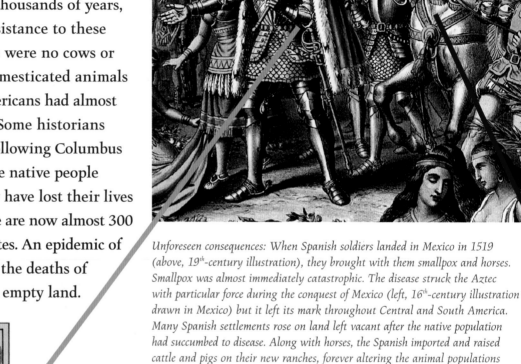

Unforeseen consequences: When Spanish soldiers landed in Mexico in 1519 (above, 19th-century illustration), they brought with them smallpox and horses. Smallpox was almost immediately catastrophic. The disease struck the Aztec with particular force during the conquest of Mexico (left, 16th-century illustration drawn in Mexico) but it left its mark throughout Central and South America. Many Spanish settlements rose on land left vacant after the native population had succumbed to disease. Along with horses, the Spanish imported and raised cattle and pigs on their new ranches, forever altering the animal populations of the Americas and creating important new commodities.

1600s. Smallpox, moving from tribe to tribe, devastates native North Americans.

1721. First experiments with smallpox inoculation in Boston.

Smallpox

1500	1600	1700	1800	1900

1540s–70s. Measles and other diseases, such as typhus, deplete local populations in Central and South America.

1677-78. Smallpox in Boston kills 205 of the town's population.

1775-82. Smallpox epidemic sweeps North America, taking 100,000 lives.

1837. Smallpox outbreak among the Plains Indians.

1979. World Health Organization announces elimination of smallpox.

1526. Smallpox spreads through Central America and reaches Peru. It may be the cause of Inca Emperor Huayna Capac's untimely death, which led to civil war among his heirs and made Pizarro's conquest in 1532 much easier.

1519. Smallpox crosses the Atlantic with Hernán Cortés and kills many Aztec in Mexico. Typhus fever is also possibly brought to the Americas by Cortés (it may have already been known to the Aztec and some Indian tribes in Mexico).

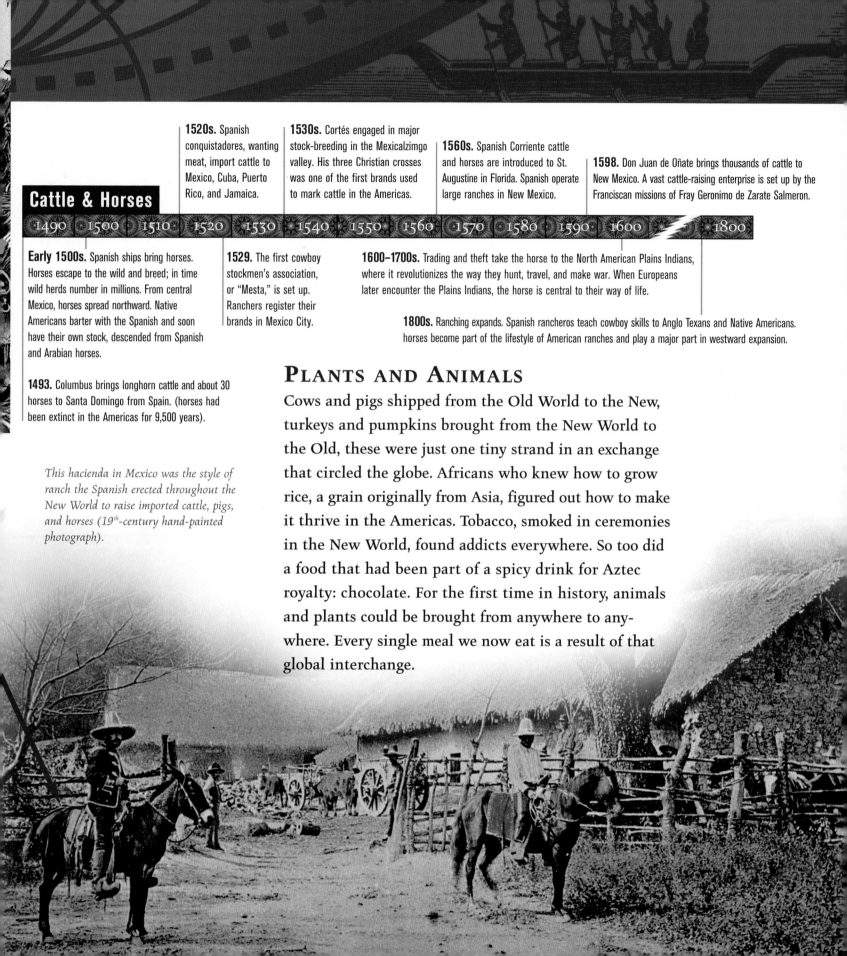

Cattle & Horses

1520s. Spanish conquistadores, wanting meat, import cattle to Mexico, Cuba, Puerto Rico, and Jamaica.

1530s. Cortés engaged in major stock-breeding in the Mexicalzimgo valley. His three Christian crosses was one of the first brands used to mark cattle in the Americas.

1560s. Spanish Corriente cattle and horses are introduced to St. Augustine in Florida. Spanish operate large ranches in New Mexico.

1598. Don Juan de Oñate brings thousands of cattle to New Mexico. A vast cattle-raising enterprise is set up by the Franciscan missions of Fray Geronimo de Zarate Salmeron.

1490 · 1500 · 1510 · 1520 · 1530 · 1540 · 1550 · 1560 · 1570 · 1580 · 1590 · 1600 · 1800

Early 1500s. Spanish ships bring horses. Horses escape to the wild and breed; in time wild herds number in millions. From central Mexico, horses spread northward. Native Americans barter with the Spanish and soon have their own stock, descended from Spanish and Arabian horses.

1493. Columbus brings longhorn cattle and about 30 horses to Santo Domingo from Spain. (horses had been extinct in the Americas for 9,500 years).

1529. The first cowboy stockmen's association, or "Mesta," is set up. Ranchers register their brands in Mexico City.

1600–1700s. Trading and theft take the horse to the North American Plains Indians, where it revolutionizes the way they hunt, travel, and make war. When Europeans later encounter the Plains Indians, the horse is central to their way of life.

1800s. Ranching expands. Spanish rancheros teach cowboy skills to Anglo Texans and Native Americans. horses become part of the lifestyle of American ranches and play a major part in westward expansion.

This hacienda in Mexico was the style of ranch the Spanish erected throughout the New World to raise imported cattle, pigs, and horses (19th-century hand-painted photograph).

PLANTS AND ANIMALS

Cows and pigs shipped from the Old World to the New, turkeys and pumpkins brought from the New World to the Old, these were just one tiny strand in an exchange that circled the globe. Africans who knew how to grow rice, a grain originally from Asia, figured out how to make it thrive in the Americas. Tobacco, smoked in ceremonies in the New World, found addicts everywhere. So too did a food that had been part of a spicy drink for Aztec royalty: chocolate. For the first time in history, animals and plants could be brought from anywhere to any-where. Every single meal we now eat is a result of that global interchange.

POPULATION

HOW MANY PEOPLE LIVED IN THE AMERICAS IN 1491?

Older history books state that, outside of the Aztec and Inca empires, the Americans were scattered across two largely empty continents. More recently, some scholars have suggested just the opposite: the Americas may have been filled with bustling villages. If this new view is true, the consequences of the Age of Exploration were the greatest tragedy in human history. We know that, after 1492, many Americans died. But does that mean millions, tens, or even hundreds of millions of people? Answering this question is like trying to solve a complex puzzle without any of the key pieces.

Drawn in the 1500s, this picture shows how some Native Americans treated the dead. Unlike Europeans, who bury the dead underground, the Algonquin believed in placing the dead on raised platforms. Since they were left exposed to animals and the elements, very few of these pre-1492 remains have been found.

French soldiers battle Timacua Indians in Florida in 1565 (16ᵗʰ-century illustration). Before the Europeans arrived, wars between the peoples of North America were often raids in which small numbers of warriors clashed. Europeans were more used to full-scale battles. And as native peoples lost their land, they clashed with their neighbors, setting off new wars. Not only did many men die, but the many conflicts often made it difficult to hunt or bring in harvests. Weakened groups were all the more likely to fall victim to disease.

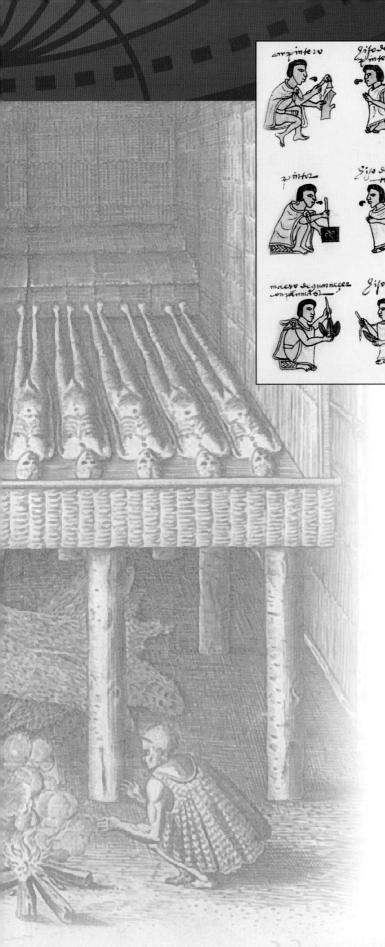

This page from the Codex Mendoza (created in 1540–41) shows the various jobs that young Aztec men were expected to learn, such as being a carpenter, painter, metalworker, or featherworker. Based on an image like this, one might estimate how many people it would take to feed those who did all of these jobs, and then how large their families might be. But those are just guesses. After all, this shows the kinds of work Aztec did, not how many men did each job.

Today, every government keeps a record of how many people live within its borders. But some people do not fill out their census forms, and statisticians have to guess at the missing numbers. In the Americas, no one counted the population, so everything is a guess. Still there is some evidence: the Spanish kept population records in parts of Mexico. If we multiply those numbers to cover all the Aztec lands, we have a place to start. The descriptions left by the very first European explorers can be used to estimate other populations. But these estimates quickly turn into guesses. By one measure, for example, the island of Hispaniola housed 200,000 people, and by another, 8 million.

The low counters ask a simple question: What happened to all the bodies? If so many millions died from 1500 on, wouldn't we find massive graveyards or at least mounds of bones? The high counters say many Americans did not bury their dead but left bodies on raised platforms, exposed to wind, rain, and animals. Right now, we have far more questions about the New World population than answers. But that is good—at one time we had only wrong answers.

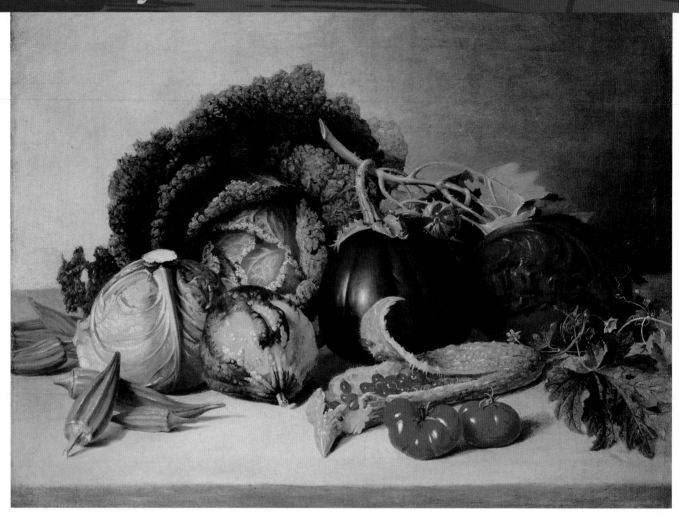

DINNER

When a Spaniard sat down to eat dinner in the Mexican port city of Veracruz, every bite was a product of the world made new. A local fish, say a red snapper, would be cooked in olive oil with garlic and onions, just as in Spain. That part of the recipe dated back to the cooking of ancient Rome, with perhaps a few flourishes added by North African Muslims. But the tomatoes and hot peppers in the recipe were pure American. Just outside his doors, slaves would be mashing the plantains originally brought from Africa. Today, fried plantains are served with the fish in a truly global dish.

This painting from the 1820s by American artist James Peale perfectly illustrates the world made new. The squash and tomatoes are native to the Americas, okra to Africa, the two kinds of cabbage to the area around the Mediterranean Sea in Europe, the eggplant to India, and the balsam apple (to left of the tomatoes; not an apple at all) is found in parts of Asia and Australia. Thus in this one still life are products of the entire world. It is this exchange of plants and animals that the Age of Exploration made possible.

GLOBAL GOLD

Global currency: Spanish silver coin with a bust of King Carlos IV. Because the Spanish spent so much money in Asia, this coin, minted in Lima, Peru, in 1792, and then transported to Spain, became legal currency in China in the late 18th and early 19th centuries, where it was known as the "Buddha-Head" coin.

In 1491, Europeans could only get the gold and silver they needed by trading with the Muslims—whose gold came from trading with Africans. When Columbus sailed, the Europeans were actually shorter of silver than gold. In the next century and half, 181 tons of gold and an astonishing 16,000 tons of silver flooded into Europe from the New World. Now Europeans had less need of Muslim gold, which hurt the caravan trade across the Sahara. But the newly wealthy Europeans could afford silks and other luxuries from the East, which led to an expansion of trade with Asia. Once again, changes that began with Columbus altered the economies of the entire world.

The route followed by the Spanish treasure ships from Peru to Cadiz, Spain, is traced in pure gold on this lavish map from 1544.

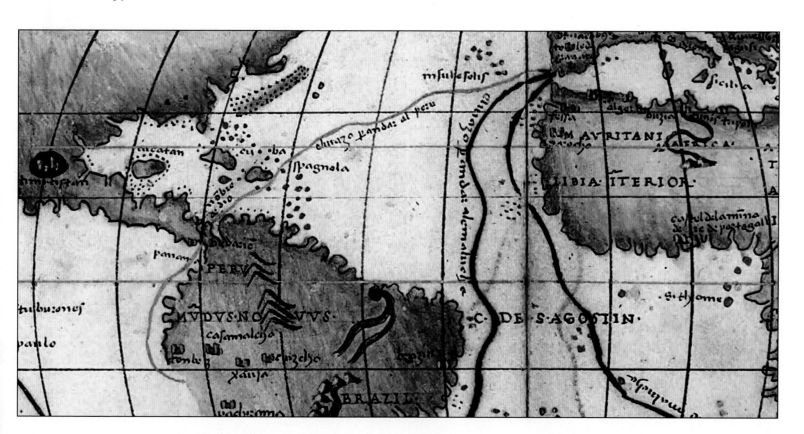

MIGRATION

Ever since the first human beings left Africa, we have been on the move. But only rarely have whole populations left one region and relocated to another. From 1492 on, that began to change. Some 12 to 13 million people were taken from Africa across the Atlantic, as slaves. Another 2 to 3 million Africans were taken by land to be sold in the Middle East. The European migration to the Americas was slower, since people chose to come and had to pay for their passage. But the Atlantic, which had been a barrier, became an open door, drawing people from throughout Europe. Within the Americas, natives were forced out of their homelands or moved to get away from the Europeans, settling in new territory. More and more people now lived far from the lands of their ancestors.

Women carry coal onto a steamship in Kingston, Jamaica, a job critical to the 19th-century Caribbean economy (19th-century painting). By the late 1800s, the native peoples of the Caribbean had been overwhelmed by the new arrivals. French, Spanish, and English colonists, along with the many descendents of African slaves, had created a truly global meeting (and mixing) place, connected by trade to every corner of the world.

1510. Leonardo da Vinci invents the water turbine.

1532. Niccolò Machiavelli's *The Prince* is published, which describes the principles by which a ruler may gain and hold power.

1492. Columbus makes landfall in the New World, ushering in the great Age of Exploration. *(See page 22.)*

1512. Copernicus proposes the theory that the Earth revolves around the sun.

Advances in Knowledge

1490	1500	1510	1520	1530

1492. First globe is built by geographer Martin Behaim.

1507. Martin Waldseemüller's world map is the first to show the New World. *(See endpapers.)*

1517. Martin Luther publishes his 95 theses, beginning the Reformation.

1516. Sir Thomas More publishes *Utopia*.

Woodcut by Ambrosius Holbein for a 1518 edition of Sir Thomas More's Utopia; *in the lower left-hand corner, a traveler describes the island of Utopia, whose layout appears above. Utopia is a philosophical work in which More imagines an ideal place and discusses what it might be like. More was inspired by the great voyages and expeditions of his time—in fact, in his book, the island of Utopia is discovered during a voyage to the Americas.*

IDEAS

The fact that Columbus found new land beyond the end of the old maps was as startling as the actual nature of the New World. For centuries Europeans had believed that the Bible, and the surviving ideas of the ancients, contained all that there was to know. Every ship returning to port now announced that there were new and unexpected things to be discovered. New ideas about religion, about the place of the sun in the sky, about everything from why an apple falls to the nature of the air we breathe followed. A New World showed that it was possible to see the world anew.

1580. French essayist Michel de Montaigne publishes *On Cannibals*, in which he uses reports of cannibalism among some native peoples in the New World to reflect on European society.

1540　1550　1560　1570　1580　1590　1600

1569. Geographer and mapmaker Gerardus Mercator creates the first modern map projection, accurately depicting the spherical planet on a flat map.

1590. Galileo Galilei conducts experiments in gravity.

1600. The telescope is invented in the Netherlands.

WAYS OF LIVING

Though the Americas were the scene of war, conquest, and enslavement, they were also a place where peoples and cultures mixed and took on new forms. The horse was one of the great advantages Spanish armies had in fighting against the Aztec and the Inca. As horses bred in America and escaped, North American natives mastered riding them and using them to hunt.

Because the Americas were far from Europe, people could experiment with ideas and customs that were forbidden at home. The women of Lima, for example, adopted a Muslim style of dress in order to add a bit of mystery, intrigue, and fashion to their clothing. The New World was not only a new location for Europeans and Africans but also a place in which all the peoples of the world experimented with new ways of living.

In this painting by the American artist Mary Cassatt from 1894, a woman plays the banjo. As Thomas Jefferson wrote in 1781, the "banjar" came to America "from Africa." For enslaved people, the banjo was a link back to their heritage. But it also became a popular instrument for Americans of all backgrounds. From the songs we sing to the foods we eat, American life is the product of this kind of mixture.

A visitor to Lima, Peru in the 16th century would immediately notice a strange fashion. The Catholic women wore tapadas, black silk shawls that completely covered their heads, leaving only one eye free, as shown in this 19th-century print. They were borrowing the head covering worn by religious Muslim women—but not as a sign of faith. In fact the Catholic church did not like the fashion at all, as it allowed women to disguise themselves and be all the more flirtatious. In the New World, customs and practices from throughout the planet were combined in new ways.

Sioux Indian Chiefs (photograph ca 1905). This is how North American Indians are often pictured: astride a horse with a rifle in hand. But the native peoples of the Americas only saw horses for the first time in the 1500s, with the arrival of the Spanish. Rifles arrived from Europe in the 18th century. The Indian on horseback was as much a product of the world joined as were the armies he opposed.

CONCLUSION

What would it be like if we woke up one morning to see fleets of giant space ships filling the skies? The arrival of visitors from a distant galaxy would challenge everything we think and believe. All the more so if they landed with machines and animals we could not understand, and if they set off waves of disease we could not explain. The shock of that encounter would be felt everywhere on earth. And yet, for the first time we would be linked to that far solar system. We and they would form a kind of bridge across the universe, and who knows what we, together, might create?

We can imagine this story out of science fiction because it really happened. The Spaniards with their sailing ships, horses, muskets, and germs were no less foreign to the peoples of the Americas than space aliens would be to us. All the more remarkable, then, that the Aztec noblewoman Malinche quickly learned Spanish and could translate for Cortés. All the more astonishing that Africans ripped out of their homelands and dropped into the Americas invented ways to live and prosper. All the more inspiring that men of conscience, such as the Spanish priest Bartoleme De Las Casas, devoted themselves to defending the Americans from other Spaniards.

The story of the Age of Exploration is, in the end, about being human. Faced with a situation that was impossible to comprehend, some responded with greed, with violence, with fear. But others recognized this as a moment for invention, for creation, for compassion. They found a way to be human in a situation no human being had ever faced. They were the true heroes of the age.

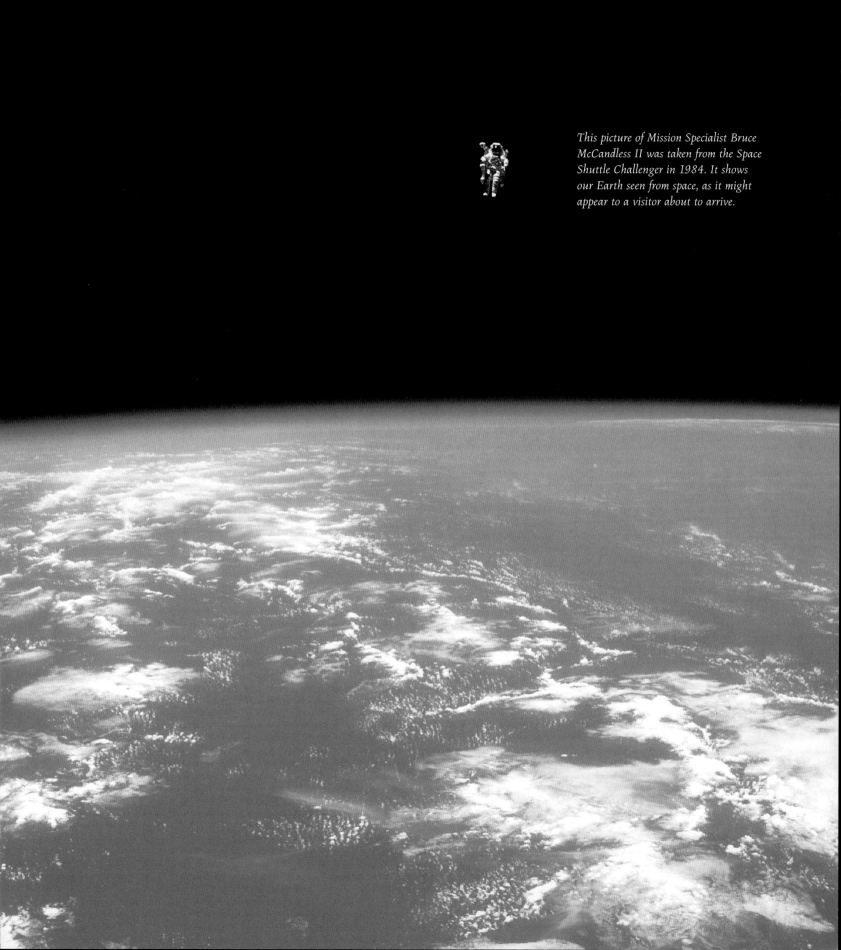

This picture of Mission Specialist Bruce McCandless II was taken from the Space Shuttle Challenger in 1984. It shows our Earth seen from space, as it might appear to a visitor about to arrive.

PLACE-FINDER MAP

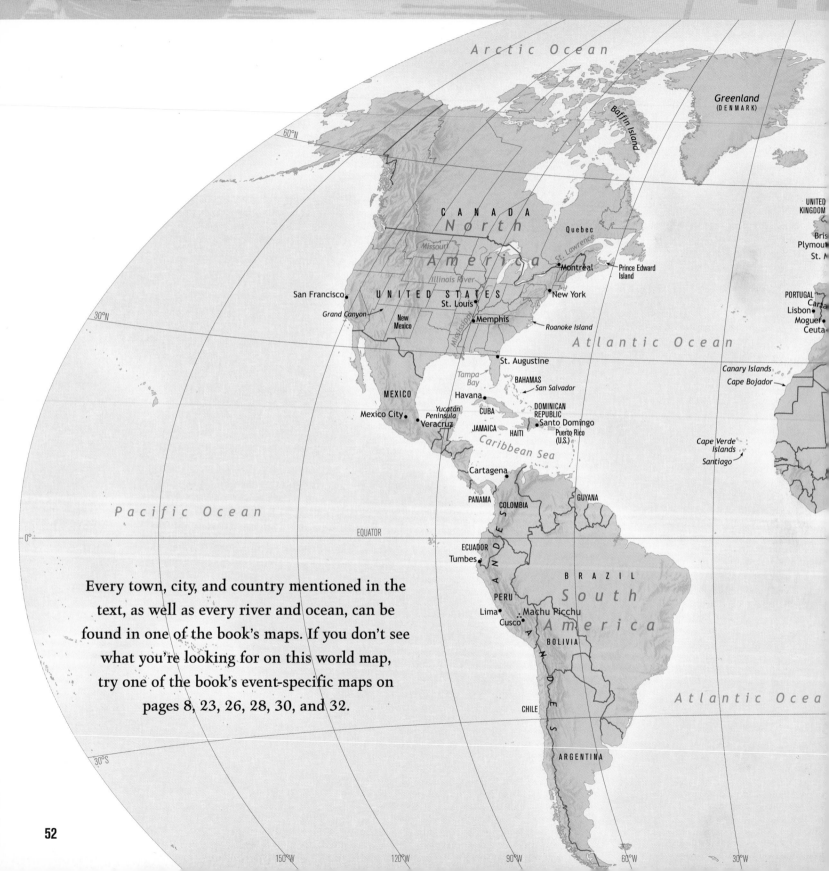

Arctic Ocean

Greenland
(DENMARK)

Baffin Island

60°N

CANADA

North

Quebec

Missouri

St. Lawrence

America

Montreal

Prince Edward
Island

Illinois River

San Francisco

UNITED STATES

New York

St. Louis

30°N

Grand Canyon

New
Mexico

Memphis

Roanoke Island

Mississippi

Atlantic Ocean

St. Augustine

Tampa
Bay

BAHAMAS

San Salvador

MEXICO

Havana

Mexico City

Yucatán
Peninsula

CUBA

DOMINICAN
REPUBLIC

Veracruz

JAMAICA

HAITI

Santo Domingo

Puerto Rico
(U.S.)

Caribbean Sea

Cartagena

Pacific Ocean

PANAMA

COLOMBIA

GUYANA

EQUATOR

0°

ECUADOR

Tumbes

BRAZIL

South

PERU

America

Lima

Machu Picchu

Cusco

BOLIVIA

ANDES

Every town, city, and country mentioned in the
text, as well as every river and ocean, can be
found in one of the book's maps. If you don't see
what you're looking for on this world map,
try one of the book's event-specific maps on
pages 8, 23, 26, 28, 30, and 32.

CHILE

30°S

ARGENTINA

Atlantic Ocea

UNITED
KINGDOM

Bris
Plymou
St. M

PORTUGAL

Carta

Lisbon

Moguer

Ceuta

Canary Islands

Cape Bojador

Cape Verde
Islands

Santiago

Atlantic Ocean

150°W   120°W   90°W   60°W   30°W

Arctic Ocean

Europe

AUSTRIA Vienna

ITALY

Rome

Mediterranean Sea

Sicily   Battle of Lepanto

Istanbul (Constantinople)

TURKEY

SYRIA

60°N

Asia

JAPAN

CHINA

Nanjing

East China Sea

30°N

EGYPT

HARA

frica

Hormuz

Arabian Peninsula

INDIA

Arabian Sea

Bay of Bengal

Calicut   Sri Lanka

South China Sea

PHILIPPINES   Mactan

Pacific Ocean

Mombasa

EQUATOR

INDONESIA

Sumatra

Java

0°

Indian Ocean

MOZAMBIQUE

Madagascar

Australia

30°S

miles

0   1,000   2,000   3,000

0   1,000   2,000   3,000

kilometers

Present-day political boundaries are shown.
Historical names appear in parentheses.

53

30°E   60°E   90°E   120°W   150°W

BIOGRAPHICAL DICTIONARY

Atahualpa (ca 1502–1533) Atahualpa became the emperor of the Inca after he defeated his half brother Huascar in battle. But even as he conquered his rival, the Spanish under Francisco Pizarro arrived in Peru. Pizarro captured and then executed the Inca ruler. *See pages 28–29.*

Vasco Nuñez de Balboa (1475–1519) As a teenager in the Spanish port city of Moguer, Balboa heard reports from sailors about the New World. In 1501, he sailed across the Atlantic. Twelve years later, he led an expedition across Panama, where he was the first European to see the Pacific from the Americas. A rival Spaniard tried and executed him on false charges. *See pages 12 and 24.*

John Cabot (ca 1451–ca 1498) Cabot was born in Italy but convinced England's Henry VIII to sponsor his search for a way across the Atlantic to Asia. Cabot first sailed in 1497, reached North America and returned to Europe. The next year he sailed again, and disappeared somewhere in what is now Canada. *See pages 24–25.*

Huayna Capac (birth year unknown, died 1527) Huayna Capac was the 11th Sapa Inca (supreme ruler) of the Inca empire, centered around present-day Peru. During his reign (1493–1527), he greatly expanded the territory controlled by the Inca through constant war with his neighbors, moving south into present-day Chile and Argentina and north into Ecuador and Colombia. His death in 1527 from smallpox sparked a power struggle between his sons, 25-year-old Atahualpa and 21-year-old Huascar. *See pages 28–29.*

Jacques Cartier (1491–1557)

Cartier was born in France and led three voyages to America for the French. On his second voyage, he founded Quebec. Though his hopes of finding gold were not realized, he pointed the French toward the area they would continue to explore and settle. *See pages 24, 30–31.*

Christopher Columbus (1451–1506)

Older books claim that Columbus was born in Genoa, Italy. That is now in some doubt. We do know that he sailed from Spain on August 3, 1492. After returning with news of gold, he led a convoy of 17 ships again the next year. The trip was less successful and not until 1498 did he cross the ocean again. His fourth and last voyage began in 1502. He died in Spain in 1506. *See pages 7–10, 21–23.*

Francisco Vázquez de Coronado (1510–54)

Born to a noble family in Spain, Coronado came to Mexico in 1535. Hearing tales of seven wealthy cities in North America inspired Coronado to organize a large expedition to find them. Between 1540 and 1542, he led 1,400 men on a lengthy trek that cost most of them their lives and yielded no gold. He died in Mexico City. *See page 33.*

Hernán Cortés (ca 1485–1547)

Determined to join in the exploration of the New World, Cortés sailed from Spain in 1504, when he was not yet 20. Seven years later he joined in the conquest of Cuba. He went on to defeat the Aztec and become captain-general of New Spain. He eventually returned to Spain, where he died. *See pages 24, 26–27.*

Bartolome De Las Casas (1474–1566)

As a child in Spain, De Las Casas saw Columbus march through Seville with seven captured Tainos. He went on to devote his life to cause of the native peoples of America. Most famously, in 1550 he made the strongest case that they were human, and deserved to be treated as well as any Christian. *See page 50.*

BIOGRAPHICAL DICTIONARY

Sir Francis Drake (ca 1543–96) A daring captain and skilled sailor, Drake served the interests of England by attacking the Spanish in America as a kind of pirate. In 1577 he set off on a voyage around the world that may have taken him all along the coast of California—his exact route is not certain. Drake died of disease off the coast of Panama. *See pages 34–35.*

King Ferdinand of Aragon (1452–1516) and **Queen Isabella of Castille** (1451–1504) The marriage of these cousins linked two rival Spanish kingdoms. Under their leadership, the

Spanish Christians defeated the Muslims who still controlled Granada, and set out to remove all non-believers from their lands. *See pages 7 and 9–10.*

Martin Frobisher (ca 1535–94) A skilled sailor, Frobisher set out in search of northern passage to Asia, over the Americas. Though he failed (and the gold he thought he had found proved not to be valuable) he helped to map what is now Canada. Along with Drake and Ralegh, he was one of the "English Sea Dogs" who challenged Spanish control of the seas. *See page 25.*

Vasco Da Gama (1460–1524) Da Gama was a Portuguese captain whose 1497–99 voyage around Africa to India was a crucial part of the Age of Exploration. By establishing a sea route to Asia, he gave Portugal the opportunity to earn great wealth, and set up a frenzy of competition among other nations to explore the oceans. *See pages 8 and 13.*

Zheng He (1371–1435) After 28 years, from 1405–33, this great Chinese Muslim sailor led seven fleets on voyages of trade and exploration. He and his ships toured southeast Asia down to what is now Indonesia, rounded India, and reached both modern Saudi Arabia and the eastern coast of Africa. *See page 8.*

Prince Henry ("the Navigator") of Portugal (1394–1460) When Henry was a young man, Europeans knew little about Africa below the Sahara. He sent out the ships that mapped its western coast. Henry is often credited with creating a "school" which gathered crucial knowledge about maps and sailing and made the Age of Exploration possible. *See pages 8, 9, and 13.*

Juan Ponce de León (ca 1460–1521) Born in Spain, Ponce de León sailed with Columbus on his second voyage to America. He is best-known for his exploration of what is now Florida. But in his day, the most important result of his voyages was the discovery of a strong ocean current (the Gulf Stream) that could speed ships across the Atlantic to Cuba and Florida. *See pages 24–25.*

Ferdinand Magellan (1480–1521) Though born in Portugal, Magellan undertook his famous effort to sail around the world under the Spanish flag. Like Columbus, he was trying to prove that he could reach Asia by sailing across the Atlantic. One of his three ships did complete the trip, but Magellan did not— he was killed in the Philippines. *See page 24.*

Malinche (ca 1502 or 1505–ca 1530) The daughter of native leaders, she may have, nevertheless, been sold into slavery, then given to Hernán Cortés as a gift. She learned Spanish quickly and proved invaluable to Cortés as a translator and perhaps strategist. Some Mexicans view her as a strong woman ancestor, others as a traitor. *See page 26.*

BIOGRAPHICAL DICTIONARY

Montezuma (ca 1480–1520) Montezuma was a scholar who was chosen by a counsel of nobles to be the ruler of the Aztec. He succeeded Ahuitzotl, who was a particularly aggressive and bloodthirsty ruler. Montezuma tried to bribe the invading Spanish, who found easy allies among natives who hated the Aztec. He was killed by his own people. *See pages 26–27.*

Pachakuti, or "Worldshaker" (birth year unknown, died 1471) When Pachakuti became Sapac Inca (or supreme ruler) in 1438, the Inca were a tribe living around the town of Cusco in present-day Peru. By his death in 1471, after years of aggressive war, the Inca were the rulers of the Andes Mountains. The Inca Empire would continue to expand until the arrival of Francisco Pizarro in 1530. *See page 16.*

Francisco Pizarro (1475–1541) Born in Spain, Pizarro sailed to the New World in 1502 and prospered. Twenty years later, he began to hear rumors of a wealthy kingdom and, in 1530, set out to find and conquer it. Fortunately for him, the Inca were in the midst of a civil war, made worse by a smallpox outbreak. Pizarro and just 180 men conquered the Inca, but he was eventually killed by a rival Spanish faction. *See pages 24 and 28–29.*

Sir Walter Ralegh (ca 1554–1618) Born near the coast of England, Ralegh was related to Francis Drake and throughout his life he was drawn to explore overseas. Though his two  trips to search for El Dorado in South America, and the colony he sponsored in North America, failed, his writings pointed the way British settlement in North America. *See page 35.*

Hernando de Soto (ca 1500–1542) Born in Spain, De Soto was known for his key role in serving with Pizarro in his conquest of the Inca. In 1539, believing that there were more rich kingdoms to be conquered, he set out on a new expedition with over 600 men. Marching from Florida across the southeast, he left behind a legacy of cruelty and destruction. He was said to have been buried near the Mississippi River. *See pages 24 and 32–33.*

Giovanni da Verrazano (ca 1485–1528) Though he was born near Florence, Italy, Verrazano sailed to the New World in service to the king of France. He was the first European to explore the area that would become New York Harbor, as well as Narragansett Bay. He was killed on a later trip, in the Caribbean. *See page 24.*

Andes Mountains: A mountain range in South America running approximately 4,500 miles north to south along the Pacific coast.

astrolabe: A navigational instrument of ancient origin that measured the height of the sun or a star from the horizon and enabled a traveler to calculate his position.

barter: To trade, usually by exchanging one commodity for another.

cartographer: Someone who makes maps, a mapmaker.

ca: An abbreviation of the word "circa," which means "around" or "about" or "approximately." This is often used with dates when a precise date is not known.

codex: An ancient book, usually written and illustrated by hand.

census: A complete count of the population. The United States government conducts a census every 10 years.

conquistador: In Spanish, "one that conquers." In the 16th century, military leaders of the Spanish conquest of the Americas, such as Hernán Cortés and Francisco Pizarro, were called conquistadores.

crossbreeding: The creation of a new hybrid breed by mixing or "crossing" two varieties within the same species.

Crusades: Military expeditions launched by European Christians in the 11th, 12th, and 13th centuries against Muslims and others seen as enemies.

epidemic: An outbreak of an extremely contagious disease or condition that quickly affects a large number people at the same time.

fountain of youth: According to legend, there was a spring or fountain in a land called "Bimini," rumored to be somewhere in the Caribbean, which could cure illnesses. Neither the spring nor the land actually existed.

llama: Related to the camel, llamas are long-necked, long-eared, hoofed animals native to South America. The peoples of the Andes Mountains rely on llamas for wool, milk, meat, and as pack animals.

Marco Polo (1254-1324): A merchant from Venice, Polo traveled through Asia to China. The book describing his travels gave Europeans their first picture of life in Asia.

migration: Moving from one location or country to another.

mosque: A place of worship for Muslims, as a church is for Christians.

Muslims: A believer in Islam, a religion that accepts the Jewish and Christian bible, but believes the prophet Mohammed brought new and final revelations.

Ottoman Empire: A vast kingdom stretching from North Africa far into Europe governed by Muslim Turks, it began in the 1200s, and lasted until 1918.

ply: To travel in a frequent and familiar route.

privateer: A pirate ship whose crew has agreed to fight for one country against another.

rancid: Having a terrible taste or smell.

Sapa Inca (supreme ruler): Title given to the head of the Inca Empire, to whom none could compare.

sea quadrant: A device invented in the mid-15th century that allowed sailors to figure out where they were on the sea at night.

Seven Cities of Cibola: Legendary cities filled with riches beyond imaging, pursued by Spanish adventurers in the 16th century in what is now the southwestern United States. The cities—and their treasures—were never found.

staple (food): The main part of something, often the main part of a diet. For example, corn was a staple of the diet of native people in North America in the 1600s.

Tenochtitlán: Capital city of the Aztec empire, founded ca A.D. 1325 on an island in Lake Texcoco. After destroying much of the city in 1521, Hernán Cortés built a new city over the ruins— Mexico City, the present-day capital of Mexico.

typhus fever: Transmitted by lice, and therefore often caused by overcrowding, this is a severe infectious disease, whose victims can suffer high fever, headache, delirium, and a red rash.

SOURCES & WEB SITES

Sources We Consulted

For an overview of the Age of Exploration, any adult library will have well-researched books by such famous historians as Samuel E. Morison or David Quinn. Not only are their works full of basic facts and information, they are also vividly written. That is also true of Hugh Thomas, who has made the history of Spanish exploration and settlement of the Americas a special focus of his recent books *Rivers of Gold* and *Conquest*. In the pages of these magisterial books you will meet every major actor, both European and American, in the early history of Spain in the New World.

We returned again and again to Zvi Dor-Ner's *Columbus and the Age of Discovery*, both for its incisive portraits of the world before and after Columbus and its extraordinary collection of period maps, illustrations, and paintings.

William H. Goetzmann and Glyndwr Williams's *The Atlas of North American Exploration* presents excellent summaries of the exploits of the important sailors and adventurers who first explored North America, accompanied by clearly presented and visually pleasing maps of their routes of exploration. Similarly, W.P. Cumming, R.A. Skelton, and D.B. Quinn's *The Discovery of North America* provides lively summaries of most of the major explorations of North America as well as extracts from the explorers' published accounts. This book also contains an outstanding collection of antique maps and period illustrations.

While we used such books to establish basic facts, our approach to *The World Made New* was strongly influenced by two recent books: *Guns, Germs, and Steel* by Jared Diamond and *1491* by Charles Mann. Both books point out how much new and interesting thought is taking place about the history of the Americas. We urge readers curious about some of the new ideas presented in our book to read Diamond and Mann. Finally, young readers can find out more about some of the ideas we present in Patricia Lauber's *Who Came First? New Clues to Prehistoric Americans* (Washington, DC: National Geographic Books, 2003).

Fernand Braudel, *The Structures of Everyday Life* (New York: Harper & Row, 1981).

W.P. Cumming, R.A. Skelton, and D.B. Quinn, *The Discovery of North America* (New York: American Heritage, 1972).

Jared Diamond, *Guns, Germs, and Steel: The Fates of Human Societies* (New York: Norton, 1997).

Zvi Dor-Ner, *Columbus and the Age of Discovery* (New York: William Morrow, 1991).

William H. Goetzmann and Glyndwr Williams, *The Atlas of North American Exploration; From the Norse Voyages to the Race to the Pole* (New York: Prentice Hall, 1992).

Bernard Grun, *The Timetables of History* (New York: Simon and Schuster, 1982).

John Haywood, *Historical Atlas of the Early Modern World 1492–1783* (New York: Barnes & Noble Books, 2002).

John Hemming, *The Conquest of the Incas* (Orlando, FL: Harcourt Brace, 1970).

Bernard Lewis, *What Went Wrong? The Clash Between Islam and Modernity in the Middle East* (New York: HarperCollins, 2003).

Charles C. Mann, *1491: New Revelations of the Americas Before Columbus* (New York: Knopf, 2005).

Samuel E. Morison, *The European Discovery of America; the Northern Voyages 1500–1600* (New York: Oxford University Press, 1971).

Jake Page, *In the Hands of the Great Spirit: The 20,000-Year History of American Indians* (New York: Free Press, 2004).

Kenneth Pomeranz and Steven Topik, *The World That Trade Created* (New York: M.E. Sharpe, 1999).

David Quinn, *North America From Earliest Discovery to First Settlements* (New York: Harper & Row, 1977).

R.A. Skelton, *Decorative and Printed Maps of the 15th to 18th Centuries* (London: Staples Press, 1952).

Hugh Thomas, *An Unfinished History of the World* (London: Pan Books, 1981).

Hugh Thomas, *Conquest: Montezuma, Cortés, and the Fall of Old Mexico* (New York: Touchstone, 1995).

Hugh Thomas, *Rivers of Gold* (New York: Random House, 2003).

Richard F. Townsend, *The Aztecs* (New York: Thames & Hudson, 2000).

Michael Wood, *Conquistadors* (Berkeley and Los Angeles: The University of California Press, 2000).

Additional Sources

We discuss below resources that may be useful to readers interested in learning more about specific subjects discussed in *The World Made New*.

PAGES 8–9. On Zhang He, see *National Geographic*, July 2005, or http://www7.nationalgeographic.com/ngm/0507/feature2/index.html

PAGES 9–13. The themes outlined here are discussed in many books, including Jared Diamond's *Guns, Germs, and Steel* (mentioned above).

PAGE 15. Richard Townsend's *The Aztecs*, mentioned above, provides a detailed portrait of Aztec life and beliefs.

PAGES 18–19. For more information about Cahokia, see the entry below under "Web Sites for Teachers".

PAGE 22. For questions about Columbus's birth place and background see http://www.latimes.com/news/opinion/commentary/la-oe-dugard15may15,0,741966.story?coll=la-news-comment-opinions.

PAGES 26–27. Hugh Thomas's *Conquest*, mentioned above, is a detailed and engaging account of the Spanish conquest of Mexico.

PAGES 28–29. John Hemming's *The Conquest of the Incas*, mentioned above, is a detailed narrative of Pizarro's conquest.

PAGES 30–31. For more information on Jacques Cartier, visit this Web site for younger readers hosted by the Library and Archives of Canada, http://www.collectionscanada.ca/explorers/kids/h3-1320-e.html.

PAGES 32–33. The precise route of Hernando de Soto's journey through the southeast and southwest is a subject of debate. However, the writer behind this quirky Web site has tried to hike in de Soto's footsteps by using as a guide the published accounts of survivors from de Soto's army: http://www.floridahistory.com/inset44.html.

PAGES 34–35. For more on Sir Francis Drake, visit the Library of Congress's online exhibition at http://www.loc.gov/rr/rarebook/catalog/drake/drake-home.html.

PAGES 38–39. One useful source on the pre-Columbian history of Hispaniola is http://www.webster.edu/~corbetre/haiti/history/precolumbian/tainover.htm.

For more about sugar, see Sidney Mintz, *Sweetness and Power; The Place of Sugar in Modern History* (New York: Penguin, 1986) and Stuart Schwartz, ed., *Tropical Babylons, Sugar and the Making of the Atlantic World 1450–1680* (Chapel Hill, NC: University of North Carolina Press, 2004).

PAGES 40–41. New research speculates that the great killer of the native people of the Americas may not have been smallpox carried by the Spanish but a native virus. See the article "Megadeath in Mexico" at http://www.discover.com/issues/feb-06/features/megadeath-in-mexico.

Pages 44–45: For a brief introduction to the world history of Mexican food, visit: http://www.mexicanmercados.com/food/foodhist.htm.

For an academic study of silver in China, see Richard von Glahn, *Fountain of Fortune: Money and Monetary Policy in China, 1000–1700* (Berkeley: University of California Press, 1996).

PAGE 46. For useful Web sites on migration to the New World, see the entries below under "Web Sites for Teachers".

PAGE 47. A wonderful, succinct analysis of the effect of the New World on the Old can be found in J.H. Elliott, *The Old World and the New 1492–1650* (Cambridge, England: Cambridge University Press, 1970).

PAGE 48. For tapadas, women "hidden by the shawl," see http://educoas.com/Portal/bdigital/contenido/interamer/interamer_59/chap4/cityspace.aspx.

Web Sites for Young Readers

The Web sites listed below are a good place to start for younger readers interested in learning more about the people and events behind the Age of Exploration.

A Web site about the Aztec with many links designed for younger readers: http://www.rock-hill.k12.sc.us/departments/research/ancient_aztecs.htm.

A similar Web site devoted to the Inca: http://www.rock-hill.k12.sc.us/departments/research/ancientincas.htm.

And for natives in North America: http://www.rock-hill.k12.sc.us/departments/research/native_americans.htm.

Three good Web sites for finding information on explorers:

http://www.collectionscanada.ca/explorers/kids (hosted by the Library and Archives of Canada)

http://www.enchantedlearning.com/explorers/page/d/dagama.shtml

http://www.win.tue.nl/~engels/discovery/large.html

Web Sites for Teachers

In addition to the Web sites listed above, teachers may find the following useful.

A good resource to begin looking for maps, drawings, and other visual primary source materials about the Caribbean: http://www.historical-museum.org/exhibits/visions/visions.htm.

An excellent Web site related to Jared Diamond's book *Guns, Germs, and Steel* with many resources for teachers: http://www.pbs.org/gunsgermssteel.

To learn more about Cahokia, with links for teachers, visit: http://www.cahokiamounds.com/cahokia.html.

For primary sources and many links related to migrations to the United States, visit: http://www.fordham.edu/HALSALL/MOD/modsbook28.html.

A short introduction to migration to South America can be found at: http://www.tcnj.edu/~fickas3/South%20America.htm.

A fine Web site on all of the African migrations to America, forced and chosen: http://www.inmotionaame.org/home.cfm.

Finally, the Library of Congress's online archives are an amazing resource for basic historical information and digitized versions of historic documents, antiques maps, and period illustrations. A good place to start is the library's homepage, where you'll find links for teachers, librarians, and children: http://www.loc.gov/index.html.

We have viewed the Web sites discussed above but we have not explored every connection and link they offer. Readers should use these sites as starting points for their research, but should be careful to compare what they see on any site with information from reliable reference books, such as those we consulted. Where they disagree, you have an interesting question to explore.

INDEX

Illustrations are indicated by **boldface**.

Acknowledgments

The authors would like to thank our wives, Marina Bhudos and Tara George, as well as our children, Sasha and Raphael Aronson, and Leela and Maya George Glenn, for their support and encouragement; Jon Glick of mouse+tiger Design for a thoroughly enjoyable collaboration; Dr. Maricel Presilla and Dr. Richard Von Glahn for their insights on, respectively, global food and the silver trade; Jane Folger of Maplewood Memorial Library, who generously reviewed an early draft of the design concept; William R. Iseminger of Cahokia Mounds State Historic Site, who improved our understanding of Cahokia; Francis Wee of www.asiannumismatics.com, for sharing his knowledge of antique coins; Tod Olson for moral support; Amy Berkower; and, finally, the team at National Geographic, including Steve Mico, Nancy Feresten, Jennifer Emmett, Bea Jackson, Jim Hiscott, David M. Seager, Lori Epstein, Sue Macy, Jean Cantu, Priyanka Lamichhane, Carl Mehler, and Matt Chwastyk for giving us a chance to make a beautiful book.

PUBLISHED BY THE NATIONAL GEOGRAPHIC SOCIETY

John M. Fahey, Jr., **President and Chief Executive Officer**

Gilbert M. Grosvenor, **Chairman of the Board**

Nina D. Hoffman, **Executive Vice President, President of Books Publishing Group**

STAFF FOR THIS BOOK

Nancy Laties Feresten, **Vice President, Editor-in-Chief of Children's Books**

Bea Jackson, **Art Director, Children's Books**

Jennifer Emmett, **Project Editor**

Lori Epstein, **Illustrations Editor**

Rebecca Baines, **Editorial Assistant**

R. Gary Colbert, **Production Director**

Lewis R. Bassford, **Production Manager**

Vincent P. Ryan, **Manufacturing Manager**

Carl Mehler, **Director of Maps**

Matt Chwastyk, **Map Research and Production**

A BOOK BY ARONSON & GLENN LLC

Written and produced by Marc Aronson and John W. Glenn

Book design, art direction, and production by Jon Glick, mouse+tiger

While every effort has been made to verify all the factual information in this book, to trace copyright holders and to seek permission to use illustrative material, Aronson & Glenn LLC would be glad to be informed of any omissions or discrepancies so that these can be rectified in future editions.

Library of Congress Cataloging-in-Publication Data

Aronson, Marc.

A world made new : why the Age of Exploration happened and how it changed the world / Marc Aronson and John W. Glenn.

p. cm.

Includes bibliographical references and index.

ISBN-13: 978-0-7922-6454-5 (hardcover)

ISBN-13: 978-0-7922-6978-6 (lib. bdg.)

1. Discoveries in geography.   I. Glenn, John W.   II. Title.

G80.A745 2007

910.9'03--dc22

2006022091

ENDPAPERS: *Created in 1507 by German cartographer Martin Waldseemüller, this world map is the first document known to identify the lands across the Atlantic as "America." On the top of the map, he honors two great mapmakers. On the left is Ptolemy, the first great Western mapmaker, who lived around the middle of the second century A.D. On the right is Amerigo Vespucci. Vespucci, a skilled cartographer himself, had returned to Europe in 1502 after exploring the coast of South America. His first name is the basis of the word "America." Waldseemüller's map blends knowledge about the shape of the world as established by Ptolemy and the latest information brought back to Europe by Spanish and Portuguese explorers. Just 15 years after Columbus thought he'd landed in Asia, European scholars had already begun to think about the lands across the Atlantic as separate from Europe and separate from Asia. They were drawing maps of a New World, and an expanded globe—a world made new.*